CW00539236

The art of life lies in a constant readjustment to our surroundings.
Kakuzo Okakura

Kakuzo Okakura, 1862-1913. Japanese art
collector and traveller. Founder of the
Tokyo University of Fine Art. Author of
the *Book of Tea* and other publications.

Illustration from the classical Chinese
tangram puzzle involving arrangements
of the same seven pieces.

Quest for Quality: an IBM exhibition

Alan Fletcher
Poster for
Quest for Quality
exhibition designed for
IBM's new HQ
in Paris, 1983.

Fiona MacCarthy and Patrick Nuttgens

EYE FOR INDUSTRY: ROYAL DESIGNERS FOR INDUSTRY 1936–1986

Lund Humphries London in association with the Royal Society of Arts

Texts copyright © 1986 Royal Society of Arts
Illustrations copyright © 1986 as credited in the captions

First edition 1986
Published by
Lund Humphries Publishers Ltd
124 Wigmore Street London W1

in association with
The Royal Society of Arts London

on the occasion of the exhibition "Eye for Industry"
held at the Victoria & Albert Museum, London
26 November 1986–1 February 1987

ISBN 0 85331 514 0

British Library Cataloguing Publication Data

MacCarthy, Fiona
    Eye for industry : royal designers for industry 1936–1986.
    1. Design – Great Britain – History – 20th century
    I. Title   II. Nuttgens, Patrick   III. Royal Society of Arts
    IV. Victoria and Albert Museum
    745.4'4941   NK928

Designed by Derek Birdsall RDI
Made and printed in Great Britain
by Balding + Mansell Limited, Wisbech

Contents

Acknowledgments

As Master of the Faculty of Royal Designers for Industry in this its 50th anniversary year it falls to me to thank, on behalf of all my fellow RDIs, the institutional supporters and the many individuals who have helped to bring this exhibition to fruition.

First, the Faculty must thank its own parent body, the Royal Society of Arts, not just for organising the exhibition as a contribution to Industry Year but also for underwriting the costs; secondly, the Department of Trade and Industry which has provided the major share of the RSA's central funding for Industry Year; thirdly, the Royal Commission for the Exhibition of 1851 for its most generous grant; and, fourthly, we thank the Victoria and Albert Museum for providing the most appropriate showplace we could possibly have hoped for.

The individuals who must be mentioned are Fiona MacCarthy (both as Exhibition Theme Director and for her work on and writing in the catalogue); Alan Irvine RDI (Exhibition Designer) and his assistant, Charles Marsden-Smedley; Derek Birdsall RDI (Exhibition graphics and catalogue design); and for their contributions to the catalogue, Patrick Nuttgens for his masterful essay; Lord Reilly and Sir Roy Strong; Simon Tait, Andrew Nahum and Alan Bartram; and, essentially, John Taylor of Lund Humphries who has so nimbly and expertly delivered the goods in handsome published form.

At the RSA itself we must thank Christopher Lucas for having faith from the start and for his inspired choice of Joanna Thackray to organise us all so calmly and delightfully; and Mary Mullin who has looked after publicity. In the V&A's Exhibitions Department we owe much to Garth Hall and his staff and also to Graham Whiffen and Laura Trueman in the Press and Public Relations Office.

Of supreme importance to any exhibition are the lenders and I should especially like to thank them together with everyone who has given their time and good advice: Aram Designs Ltd; G. & S. Allgood Ltd; Nicholas Ardizzonne; Bath Museums Service; Beaulieu Motor Museum; Emma Beck; British Architectural Library and Drawings Collection RIBA; British Railways Board, Railways Technical Centre, Derby; British Motor Industry Heritage Trust; Fergus Chadwick; Joy Chadwick; Jennifer Chibnall; Sydney Cockerell; Laura Cohn; Concorde Lighting Ltd; Ann Crawley; Jack Daniels; Design Council – Slide Library, Sylvia Katz; Christopher Eimer; Dr David Fisher; Geffrye Museum, GEC Telecommunications Ltd; GEC Traffic Automation Ltd; Griselda Gilroy; Goldsmith's Company; Susan Hewer; Carol Hogben; Avis Hutt; Imperial War Museum; J. C. Bamford Excavators Ltd; Jaguar Cars Ltd; Neville Jason; London Transport Museum; London Regional Transport News and Photo Library; Lotus Cars Ltd; Peter Lumley; Joyce Mead; Dame Alix Meynell; E. B. Morgan; John Murray Ltd; National Film Archive; Norman Parkinson; National Portrait Gallery; The Plessey Company; Penguin Books Ltd; Jack Pritchard; RAF Museum; Rank Film Distributors; Robert Race; Sally Race; Rolls-Royce plc; Adel Rootstein; Royal Institute of Naval Architects; Royal Pavilion, Art Gallery and Museums, Brighton; Marian Russell; Pat Schleger; Tanya Schmoller; Science Museum, Aeronautical Collection, Domestic Appliances Collection, Library, Road Transport Collection; St. Bride Printing Library; Janet Stone; Thorn EMI Ferguson Ltd; Thorn EMI Lighting Ltd; Turkish Tourist Office; Victoria & Albert Museum, in particular Dr Rowan Watson, Robert Howell, Cathy Cripwell and Andrew Isherwood at the National Art Library and Archive of Art and Design, Margaret Timmers and Mark Haworth-Booth of the Department of Designs, Prints and Drawings, Stephen Astley of the Department of Furniture and Woodwork, Jennifer Hawkins Opie and Ann Eatwell of the Department of Ceramics and Glass, Eric Turner of the Department of Metalwork, Frances Hinchcliffe of the Department of Dress and Textiles; Warner & Sons; The Wedgwood Museum; Weidenfeld Archive and Library; Wilkinson Sword Ltd; Yardley & Co.

Last, but not least, I must thank my fellow Royal Designers for Industry, many of whom have lent exhibits or arranged for their loan, and without whom there would not be an exhibition.

Kenneth Grange
Master of the Faculty of Royal Designers for Industry

Introduction
Christopher Lucas, Secretary, Royal Society of Arts

The exhibition *Eye for Industry* at the Victoria and Albert Museum has been organised by the Royal Society of Arts for two reasons. First, it is a contribution to Industry Year 1986, itself an initiative of the RSA; secondly, it is a celebration of the 50th anniversary of the founding, by the RSA in 1936, of the distinction Royal Designer for Industry (RDI).

The aim of Industry Year has been "to encourage a better understanding of industry, its essential role and its service to the community, and to win acceptance for it". The level of esteem accorded to British industry is directly affected by our assessment of the quality of goods and services we produce for ourselves and overseas customers. *Eye for Industry* sets out to show, through the work of Royal Designers for Industry, that quality and integrity of purpose are inseparable ingredients in any example of true excellence in design. The exhibition also reveals how pervasive the influence of excellent design can be in terms of wealth creation and quality of life.

Foreword
Lord Reilly

It is very appropriate that this exhibition which marks fifty years of the Faculty of Royal Designers for Industry should fall in Industry Year 1986, for good design is one of British industry's outstanding needs; and if there is one attribute which is shared by all RDIs it is their conviction that quality is all-important, whether in terms of manufacture, materials, performance or vision.

It is also highly appropriate that the exhibition should be held in the Victoria and Albert Museum, that national repository of superb artifacts from all over the world and all ages. A fact not so well known is that the collection has been increasingly drawn from our own times and our own country, and thus, of course, from the drawing-boards or workshops of Royal Designers.

As the exhibition shows, the scope of work done by the RDIs as a group, or even by RDIs as individuals, is exhilarating, ranging from dresses to bridges, from railway locomotives to motor cars, from furniture to pottery, from glass to textiles, and including the graphics, displays, exhibition and other forms of publicity by which such products are promoted and sold. Fifty years ago it would have been hard to assemble a reasonable show of design, for we were still wallowing in reproductions of all kinds and shopkeepers had no idea of the changes to come; they were still regurgitating last year's successes. But that was long before the arrival on the market of the hosts of electronic gadgets, mostly, alas, imported, which have so radically changed the face of industrial design. It was also long before the High Street revolution whereby shops and stores take each other over and with each deal employ a designer to provide a new image and often to reassess the design of the merchandise on offer. There is no doubt that during the period 1936–86 covered by the exhibition the designer has come into his own and now finds himself courted by businessmen of all kinds, eagerly seeking a new identity. Indeed, this very popularity of the designer has led to the proliferation of many charlatan consultancies who vie with one another to produce the most eye-catching result. They tend to ignore the stabilising role of quality, which is why this show is so important and why it should be visited by everyone concerned with design, but particularly by those teaching at or attending business schools; for the industrial designer, unlike the craftsman, relies as much on the intelligence of his clients as on his own abilities.

The fifty years that have passed since The Royal Society for the Encouragement of Arts, Manufactures and Commerce – more familiarly the Royal Society of Arts or RSA – founded the Faculty of Royal Designers for Industry have seen enormous improvements in public appreciation of design, in the role of the designer and in the scope of his practice. Even so it must be admitted that we could still assemble as abysmal a collection of bad design as ever we could.

British industry has still to demonstrate that it has grasped the point that better design remains just about the only factor capable of providing a competitive edge. If this exhibition helps the learning curve in that respect it will be a very important contribution.

The V&A and Design

Sir Roy Strong

It is some measure of how far the V&A has travelled in the last decade in its commitment to modern design and creativity that a celebration of the 50th anniversary of the RDI should now sit so naturally within its walls. Sir Henry Cole, the first director, would have been mightily pleased.

My arrival at the V&A in 1974 coincided with a public debate on the need for a museum of modern design in this country, a debate which included an attack on the Museum for what was seen as its lamentable track record on collecting and exhibiting twentieth-century artifacts. The resolution of this problem, I realised, was to be central to my directorship as events have since proved. It meant broadening the well-established system of acquisition, in terms of "media" and "material", to embrace the creativity of this century with its fresh use of traditional materials and its exciting application of new ones. This had to go hand in hand with a shift from the attitude that objective judgements could on the whole only be made in retrospect. Two events in fact hastened this development. The first was the decision made in 1975 to allocate each department within the Museum a special purchase grant to acquire only items made after 1920. The response initially was understandably very uneven but a decade later I think that the decision can be looked back upon with some degree of satisfaction in terms of its results. The second event fell within the category of "It is an ill wind that blows . . ." namely, the closure of the Department of Circulation in 1977–78. That resulted in the transfer of their largely contemporary holdings to the departments and this greatly reinforced the urge to collect in the present as well as the past.

By the close of the 1970s there was a modernist in most departments and I am happy to write that in 1986 the situation has greatly changed from 1974. The sojourn of the Conran Foundation in the Boilerhouse from 1981–86 did much for the V&A's image as a lively centre for modern design, particularly for a younger audience. Its prime focus on industrial design was also important in sorting out the areas in which the Museum would and would not collect. That space will re-open in 1987 as our own 20th Century Exhibition Gallery with a programme which includes exhibitions on Irving Penn, Zika Ascher, Alvar Aalto, the Ferragamo shoe collection and French contemporary design. Our holdings on post-1920 artifacts have burgeoned on a vast scale. For some departments 90 per cent of their intake is now of things made in this century. We also have a British Art and Design Gallery taking the story down to 1960 whereas before it ended in 1900. More significant is the already substantial Archive of Art and Design which was instigated in 1977 and is now housed at Blythe Road. With holdings which include the papers of such figures as Sir Misha Black, a distinguished Master of the RDI, it is already proving to be a major quarry for scholars and students alike. The adoption of the subtitle "The National Museum of Art and Design" by the V&A has given us for the first time since our founding an identity which our diversity has sometimes seemed to defy. The incorporation of the word design too into some of the departmental titles has also adjusted our focus. Finally there is the establishment of the first MA course in Design and the Decorative Arts with the Royal College of Art. The latter was an offspring of the V&A in the last century and the fruitful restoration of a permanent link with a post-graduate college of art and design has given new vigour to both institutions. In addition it has been a healthy stimulus to the new discipline of design history.

Our biggest problem remains the housing and display of the modern collections. With the Trustees' appointment of Michael Hopkins as consultant architect for the entire site a master plan has been evolved which includes the construction of a new building in the courtyard behind the present entrance in Exhibition Road. That we hope to start in the early 1990s. It will require substantial funding and we trust that it will go up before the year 2000 is reached by which time our so-called modern collections will already be old and colleagues will rightly be obsessed by the artifacts of the new century. What is absolutely crucial, however, is that the V&A never again loses its continuing dialogue with the present in the terms of acquisition, display and event.

The Influence of Science and Art upon Productive Industry
Simon Tait and Andrew Nahum

The Royal Society of Arts received a special grant of £10,000 towards the costs of the *Eye for Industry* exhibition from the Royal Commission for the Exhibition of 1851

As one of their contributions to Industry Year 1986 Rolls-Royce has sponsored the exhibition *Excellence in Engineering Design* which is showing at the Science Museum, almost concurrently with *Eye for Industry*.

The connections between the institutions involved and the themes of the two exhibitions themselves must not be allowed to go unnoticed.

It is a remarkable accolade to the organisers of the Exhibition of the Works of Industry of All Nations – more familiarly the Great Exhibition of 1851 – that 135 years after it closed it remains the most popular exhibition ever. Over six million people saw it. The organisers were incorporated by Queen Victoria as the Commission for the Exhibition of 1851, and when it was all over a Supplemental Charter empowered them to remain to "increase the means of industrial education and extend the influence of science and art upon productive industry".

The 1851 Commissioners are still carrying out that directive, administering and building upon the legacy of that catalyst event, which was conceived in the Royal Society of Arts, nurtured by Prince Albert and brought to Hyde Park in Paxton's mighty greenhouse by the Commissioners and their co-opted specialists.

The 1851 Exhibition made a profit of £186,000. With it and a Government loan (repaid six years later with the aid of a mortgage) they bought 87 acres in the semi-rural village of Brompton on which to build a "locality" where they would start to fulfil the terms of their Supplemental Charter. They called it South Kensington.

East of Exhibition Road were established the South Kensington Museum, the School of Naval Architecture and Engineering (subsequently moved to Greenwich), the Royal College of Science, and the Royal College of Art on land which later passed to Government ownership to reduce the mortgage, and which became the site of the Victoria and Albert Museum.

On the main square between Kensington Road, Exhibition Road, Cromwell Road and Queen's Gate the Commissioners built their educational estate much of which remains as their freehold.

The International Exhibition of 1862 made way later for the Natural History Museum. Permanent institutions were established, including the Central Hall of Arts and Sciences (the Royal Albert Hall), the Royal College of Music, the Royal College of Organists, the Royal School of Needlework, and Queen Alexandra's House, a hostel for female students.

Later the Science and Geological Museums and the Royal College of Art were established, and several institutions were combined to become the Imperial College of Science and Technology.

The 1851 Commissioners' South Kensington estate provides income for the schemes which have been their main activity since 1891. Over the years more than 1,250 science research scholars have been appointed from the universities of the United Kingdom and the Commonwealth, 124 of whom have been elected Fellows of the Royal Society, three following Prince Albert and becoming President of the Commission. Eleven have won Nobel prizes, five Orders of Merit. The role of beneficiaries includes such names as Rutherford, Penney, Dirac and Cockcroft.

In 1985–86 the Commissioners disbursed over £300,000 in educational grants. To encourage the collaboration of engineering and industrial design, two schemes are funded, one involving collaboration between the Royal College of Art and the Imperial Institute, the other computer-aided design studies and research at the Royal College of Art. The Commissioners are also engaged in a variety of other initiatives to advance industrial education. In the *Eye for Industry* exhibition, for example, we see the Royal Society of Arts and the 1851 Commission coming together again, this time the latter assisting the former to celebrate the 50th anniversary of another important RSA initiative, namely the founding in 1936 of the Faculty of Royal Designers for Industry who can so justifiably claim to be extending – as the Commission endeavours to do – the influence of science and art upon productive industry.

The opportunity should not be lost to make another apposite – and opposite – connection. Opposite because it is to be found in the Rolls-Royce sponsored exhibition *Excellence in Engineering Design* which can be seen concurrently at the Science Museum on the other side of Exhibition Road. Apposite because here again we see the influence of science and art – though this time emphatically more of the former than the latter – upon productive industry. But what a chasm of dissension waits to open up before the feet of anyone foolhardy enough to argue a view of design from one particular per-spective! And how perfectly do these two simultaneous exhibitions, one at the Victoria and Albert Museum, the other at the Science Museum, illustrate the stupidity of attempting to separate art and science in the various design disciplines and applications.

Conceptually, we can rank industrial products on a spectrum, encompassing at one end items like cosmetic jars, where the functional constraints are minimal and where aesthetic considerations (or "appeal") outweigh almost everything else, except for cost. In the centre of the spectrum, we find articles like razors, hairdryers, hand drills and even cars, which all have to work and handle well, but where the shape differentiates the individual product from competitors using virtually identical mechanical principles. At the other end of our hypothetical spectrum, the aero engine asserts that except for the maker's sticker on the side, absolutely nothing about it is the result of aesthetic considerations. Yet who would deny that the result is a work of art?

The inseparability of art and science in the process of harnessing the productive talents of the human race for the common good was fully understood when the founders of the *Royal Society for the encouragement of Arts Manufactures and Commerce* chose their Society's name in the mid-eighteenth century and when the 1851 Commissioners set their continuing objective towards the end of the nineteenth. When we ignore their percipience we do so at our peril.

The Renaissance in British design

Patrick Nuttgens

There is a great tradition of design in Britain which is fundamental to its economic as well as its cultural life. In no country more than Britain did the complex interrelationship of ideas and manufacture result in a range of products capable of changing the environment in a positive and imaginative way. But it has been a tradition interrupted by periods of decline. Now in Industry Year it is appropriate to review the successes of design and its impact on the life of the country and explore the way in which it can contribute more.

For there are many signs of a renaissance in British design. Its products grow in popularity as much – or possibly more – abroad as at home and British designers are welcomed in many countries. And that provokes the question whether there is something distinctively British about British design.

At a time when communications are better and more immediate than ever before, it would be surprising if design characteristics did not cross national boundaries and appear all over the world. But that, although more slowly, has always been the case in history. What is distinctive is not so much a range of products as the type of product which a country needs and uses – and an attitude of mind which results in the development of a special range of skills. It is possible to identify that attitude by selecting certain moments in history when a style was specifically – or uniquely – British.

The discovery in 1320 that silver nitrate when applied to glass and fired could give a wonderful range of yellows from pale yellow to deep orange, whereas other colours had to be incorporated in the glass when molten, opened up the possibility of very flexible drawing and colour ranges. The distinctive style of glass painting that developed in the fifteenth century spread into Europe; but nowhere was it more distinctive and mature than in England. It was as if the design possibilities matched the aspirations of the English glass stainers, like John Thornton of Coventry who designed and made the great east window in York Minster. The individual scenes became smaller, the overall design more spread across the expanse of window, the drawing more sharp and cartoon-like, the borders more elaborate, the decorative canopies more imaginative, the light of the window more evenly diffused across the whole window so that it becomes a constituent part of the architecture.

And indeed the glass contributed in the fifteenth century to the style of Gothic architecture which is also distinctively English. That was the Perpendicular Style, which occurred nowhere else in Europe. It is characterised not only by the soaring verticals and closely clustered shafts of the columns which gave the name to the style when (much later) it came to be categorised, but just as effectively by the horizontals which are spaced so that the whole design becomes as compartmented as the glass. And the plans. With wider spans and flatter roofs and long uninterrupted spaces within the churches, the styles achieved a complex unity which is unmistakably English.

And just as unmistakably English – and ultimately more influential – was the eighteenth-century landscape garden. It was William Kent who (in Walpole's phrase) leapt the fence and found all nature was a garden; and his contemporary Bridgeman who probably invented the *ha-ha* or sunken fence so that the land could appear to be continuous while the cattle mysteriously stopped at a respectful distance and "no disgusting display of art" was visible. That was a phrase of Lancelot Brown, better known as Capability Brown, who more or less transformed the landscape of the British Isles. He was said to have turned down an invitation to landscape a park in Ireland on the grounds that he had not yet finished England.

The English landscape garden was known in its own time to be different from anything on the Continent. Its characteristics were the rejection of formal organisation, the lack of visible boundaries, the continuity from the house to the indefinite distance, the green swards and clumps and belts of trees so that everything would seem to be natural. It was a brilliantly organised system with controlled waters and spreading lakes, an apparently unplanned environment that was actually the result of inspired organisation. The grass would grow, the cattle would graze and nature would seem to be in a delightful equilibrium.

If so, it was an equilibrium that was shattered by an interruption of world-wide importance that had a fundamental and lasting effect. The development of a characteristic kind of British design – inspired by the countryside, unpretentious, continuous, apparently informal while actually organised, simple and yet eccentric, was complicated for ever by the phenomenon for which Britain was internationally responsible and from which it then retreated. That was the Industrial Revolution.

Between roughly 1750 and 1850 England and Scotland fostered that revolution in the affairs of men that was to change first themselves and then the whole world. But they reacted against their own success. While enthusiasts from European countries saw the Great Exhibition of 1851 and returned to their own countries to develop the manufacture and production of new artifacts, Britain seems to have retreated into its past and shrunk from the implications of mechanisation – a process that witnessed the decline of one industry after another in the twentieth century.

In effect it meant a retreat from technology. And that was odd because the word itself was one of the great inventions of the Industrial Revolution. It seems to have been coined by Beckmann, Professor of Economy in the University of Göttingen and author of the *History of Inventions*, in 1772. By the early nineteenth century it had come to mean the systematic definition (*logos*) of the rational principles upon which processes employed in the arts (*techne*) were based. It implied a systematic approach to the practical arts – what the latest edition of the *Encyclopaedia Britannica* defines as "the means or activity by which man seeks to change or manipulate his environment".

It is obvious that in such a process the activity of design is fundamental, not a superficial tidying up of a needed commodity but the very invention of the artifacts that industry is capable of producing. As early as 1835 the House of Commons set up a Select Committee on Art and Manufactures to examine why foreign manufactures were already superior to British ones. Its conclusion after receiving masses of evidence, was to recommend the setting up of Schools of Design, to produce an education of a different character from the conventional kind of schooling. "The connection of art with manufacture", the report stated, "has often developed the genius of the greatest masters of design".

Within thirty years there were over 90 schools of design in most parts of the country, especially the great manufacturing cities. The school in London which ultimately became the Royal College of Art was, like the others, founded to train designers for industry. The problem with all of them was the same – a national inclination to escape from the harsh realities of industry and commerce into the more agreeable world of art for art's sake.

The supreme – and most characteristically British – attempt to provide an answer to this predicament was one of the most colourful episodes in the history of design, doomed to partial failure but now being recognised as a major step in the development of the great tradition. That was the Arts and Crafts movement of the turn of the nineteenth and twentieth centuries. Its prophet was William Morris: "Have nothing in your houses", he wrote, "that you do not know to be useful and believe to be beautiful".

The lasting importance of the Arts and Crafts movement had a further dimension. Because it was concerned with the design and making of everyday things, like furniture and textiles and books and the decoration of ordinary rooms for ordinary people, it was forced to conclude, as happened in the case of Morris, that art could not be separated from social reform. Art, like life, was for everyman. Art could therefore stimulate social reform by being itself an answer to social problems, acting as one of the remedies in a general scene of personal responsibility. The key to it was making the artist himself responsible, as a responsible workman. And what he was to produce was Art for Everyman – what Morris called "the well making of what needs making". That of course was what we now call design.

When Hermann Muthesius, who had been an attaché at the German embassy in London, published *Das Englische Haus* in 1904 it was virtually a tribute to the Arts and Crafts movement, which had inspired probably the most complete, consistent and imaginative school of total design that England ever saw. Its leading figures – like Voysey and Lethaby and Ashbee and Mackintosh – were, it must be observed, architects. But they were also designers of everything that the architecture used or housed. The English House was one with plain walls and handsome woodwork, with well-designed textiles and glass, furniture, tiles and tapestries, knives and forks – everything big and small. And this makes a fundamental point. What ultimately characterised the movement was that the inspiration for a design might be generated by the small rather than the big. A well-designed detail could be the mainspring for a whole system of design.

In that it was the opposite of the tradition of the Beaux-Arts, in which a design started with a grand idea untrammeled by detail or thoughts of practicality and gradually resolved itself as the design was worked up and might or might not become a practical possibility. The English tradition was the other way round. The resolution of a ribbed vault in an aisle of Durham Cathedral could lead, with an exercise of the imagination, to one of the most awe-inspiring styles in the history of architecture – the Gothic. The refinement of a sash window in the eighteenth century could inspire the most civilised style of ordinary housing. The study of a timber joint or the corner of a roof or a door latch or the seat of a chair or a lock or the page of a book could lead to a humane, homely, satisfying, domestic style. For everyone – if only it could be made cheap enough.

And that, to follow the fortunes of British design, was what was expressed in the beliefs of the Design and Industries Association set up in 1915. It was directly influenced by the Deutscher Werkbund (founded by Muthesius in 1907) that aimed to bring together art and industry. The DIA's first pamphlet, which had an enthusiastic reception, stated that it aimed to encourage "a more intelligent demand among the public for what is best and soundest in design"; and it announced confidently that "the first necessity of sound design is fitness for purpose". Taking a step further than could be done by the Arts and Crafts movement with its devotion to handcraft and its hatred of the machine, the Design and Industries Association aimed "to harmonise right design and manufacturing efficiency, accepting the machine in its proper place, as a device to be guided and controlled, not merely boycotted".

With these statements, however incomplete and sometimes unrealised in the fortunes of individual members of the DIA, the approach of the designer in Britain becomes more clear: the theoretical basis increasingly insists on the meaning of design in the community and the way it affects every person.

Frank Pick was the publicity manager and then general manager of the London Underground, described later as "perhaps the outstanding example of Fitness for Purpose on a vast scale". He was a founder member of the DIA and had no doubt about the function and importance of the designer. He commissioned young artists to prepare posters for the Underground. He also approached the greatest calligrapher of the time, Edward Johnston, in 1916 and commissioned him to design a new typeface for all signs and notices. That sans-serif block letter became known internationally. An immediate descendant of it was the *sans-serif* typeface designed by Johnston's most celebrated pupil Eric Gill, which in its turn generated an international family of clear simple legible typefaces.

Design in Britain, said Pick, should be "modest and not too grandiose in scale. . . . not too logical in form . . . a reasonable compromise between beauty and utility, neither overstressing beauty till it degenerates into ornament, nor overstressing utility until it becomes bare and hard". Speaking to a meeting of the DIA in Edinburgh he pointed out that,

everything is made for a use. The test of a good thing is its fitness for that use. So that boots eked out with canvas or paper, or fashioned of porous leather, are not good, for the essence of a good boot is to keep the foot dry. So that flower-vases with narrow bottoms that topple over and make a mess are no good. So that a salt-pot in metal that corrodes with the natural dampness of the salt is no good. So that posters ornamented and confused until the words cannot be read at a glance (the minimum requirement of a poster) are no good.

The test of the goodness of a thing is its fitness for use. If it fails on this first test, no amount of ornamentation or finish will make it any better.

The achievement of Pick and the DIA was to begin to bridge the gap between craft and the machine. The fact that the best designers were now working for an underground railway rather than a back-to-the-land community was very significant. The English tradition, exemplified in the Arts and Crafts, of workshop-based handicrafts and a hatred of the abstraction fearfully entitled "the machine", took on a new realism as its leaders worked for industry and its associated activities. Eric Gill, for example, a propagandist bitterly denouncing the machine, did some of his best work when the Monotype Corporation commissioned him to design a new set of typefaces, which included the elegant and very readable classically based Perpetua and Joanna as well as Gill Sans. It was said that his thorough understanding, acquired through his lettering on a big scale, of the structure of the individual letter-form was what made him so efficient and sensitive as a type designer.

That comment was made by Gordon Russell, who was himself the paradigm of an English designer and the most successful in establishing design as a British activity. Starting as a maker of furniture in the Cotswolds, he became an exponent of the Modern Movement in design when his brother R. D. Russell, trained as an architect, joined him. But it was his two major public activities that made him the prophet of design. During World War II he accepted the challenge of making Utility furniture, starting as an exercise in economy of material and ending with a range of furniture which was generally better than the uneconomical pieces that preceded it. He aimed "to ensure that well-designed articles were available from stock".

Of his many activities the one that most affected everyone in Britain was his direction of the Council of Industrial Design after the war for more than 10 years. It was set up to promote higher standards of industrial design, was responsible for the selection and display of over 10,000 exhibits at the Festival of Britain in 1951, founded the Design Centre in London and then in other cities, *Design* magazine and the *Design Index*. Reflecting one of the central themes of the Modern Movement, he had no doubt that what was needed in design was a total re-examination of purpose, a basic need described in his own words: "If only one can state one's problem clearly it is already half-solved".

By the 1950s British design had reached a recognisable position. A hundred years of design activity and endless talk as well as two wars and the aftermath of two industrial revolutions had produced an attitude towards design which included these characteristics. Good design was concerned with everyday ordinary things; it was unpretentious, sometimes rustic in character, would reveal good craftsmanship and great competence, was vernacular (that is, local regional or national rather than international) and the product of common sense rather than unique genius. For what after all is common sense but the understanding by a community of what will work and what will not, a knowledge based on experience rather than theory?

It follows that the characteristically British approach to design is not that of the wayward genius or the isolated fantasist. For the British designer in that great tradition creativity is not something fantastic or unusual; it is part of the equipment of everyone. As an abstraction it does not of course actually exist. The English are an empirical race, working from precedent to precedent rather than general theories; the English suspicion of abstractions finds the idea of "creativity" as elusive and intangible as the idea of "originality", which may merely hide the fact that no one has been so stupid as to do it before. What makes sense to a designer and is, I believe, one of the most important factors in the renaissance of British design and manufacture is what I have elsewhere described as "creative ingenuity".

The rejection of technology was in part based upon a misunderstanding of what technology means. Technology is intimately bound up with Art – the *techne* of which the *logos* is a systematic explanation. That is what we today call design; for art has taken on since the end of the eighteenth century a special meaning which usually excludes the objectivity which is an essential element of the art of solving practical problems. Art and technology cannot be separated in an advanced technological society; "creative ingenuity" expresses the unity of art and technology essential to the process of design.

Technology at its simplest – and probably also at its most complicated – is concerned with solving other people's problems. That requires the statement of the problem (which Gordon Russell demanded), the consideration of alternatives, the elimination of the inappropriate, the following of a regular procedure and some kind of quantitative assessment. There is nothing dull about it. Creative ingenuity demands an exercise of the imagination as well as of the intellect. It requires intuition – that is, not some irrational feeling but the direct apprehension of the solution to an individual problem after exploring it in practice and in the mind. And that is exactly what the British tradition in design was famous for doing.

A vivid statement of the process at the most ordinary level is given in Robert Persig's cult book *Zen and the Art of Motorcycle Maintenance* . . .

Sometime look at a novice workman or a bad workman and compare his expression with that of a craftsman whose work you know is excellent and you'll see the difference.
The craftsman isn't following a single line of instruction. He's making decisions as he goes along. For that reason he'll be absorbed and attentive to what he's doing even though he doesn't deliberately contrive this. His motions and the machine are in a kind of harmony. He isn't following any set of written instructions because the nature of the material at hand determines his thoughts and motions, which simultaneously change the nature of the material at hand. The material and his thoughts are changing together in a progression of changes until his mind's at rest at the same time as the material's right. "Sounds like art", the instructor says. "Well, it is art", I say. This divorce of art from technology is completely unnatural. It's just that it's gone on so long you have to be an archaeologist to find out where the two separated.

In fact it does not require an archaeologist but an analytical study of the Industrial Revolution. And it will be a central achievement of Industry Year if something can be done to end the divorce between art and technology. The key to it is the understanding and use of design in manufacture. And that requires, as this exhibition will abundantly show, a serious attempt by both designers and industrialists to understand the work and aspirations of each other. There is a backlog of misunderstanding and even hostility. Sometimes, in the north of England, one gets the impression that, whatever the attitude of the designers, manufacturers would rather go into liquidation than employ a designer.

The situation is changing but above all represents a major challenge to education. The barriers between design and manufacture will not be climbed until education encourages an awareness of design at all levels – from the pupils in primary schools to the graduates in universities and polytechnics. And that requires some drastic changes in the organisation of subjects and teaching methods, crossing the boundaries between disciplines and introducing every pupil to the world of doing and making and organising.

Meantime it is worth tracing the background to an under-standing of British design because it is a great tradition which has influenced designers in many parts of the world even when they have not been aware of it. And it may be that what British design had arrived at sixty or seventy years ago has not died but is central to any new departures in design. If the Arts and Crafts attitude to design was founded upon an idea of social reform, in which good design was a central requirement for the fuller life of everyone as well as the designer, then surely we must now, in the ever-expanding ripples of the third industrial revolution, see design as central to another wave of social change affecting us all.

That can be seen in the case of architecture. Having gone through a period of disillusion with the results of the international Modern Movement, we have shifted our ground from the consensus which seemed to give us some certainty about what was right and wrong to the current pluralism where there are many answers to differently defined problems. And it could be that Britain is best at that. What we have seen is the rejection in architecture of the international modern style and its succession by a collection of styles called variously postmodernism and postmodern classicism.

If that is true of architectural design it is true of design in many other fields – Graphic Design, Furniture, Fashion, Product Design and Engineering and Environmental Design. It now seems that the influence of the Bauhaus was an aberration; the idea of a kind of design that would be all-embracing in its scope was an illusion. It was one thing to have a consistency of design from small to large in any one place; it did not follow that there should be a sameness of design in all commodities and all countries.

What Britain has to offer instead is a return not to the artifacts but to the attitudes of the turn of the century and a restatement of the great tradition of British radicalism. It means taking a ruthless look at every problem, using the full possibilities of modern technology and trying to solve each problem afresh. In the age of electronics, of information technology and the sophistication of controls, that no longer means standardisation; it means greater variety; more individualism, more idiosyncrasy, more colour, more fun.

And its supreme products will be not so much the pretentious as the everyday, the individual rather than the universal solution, variety rather than uniformity – possibly the small workshop rather than the big organisation. In a scene characterised by a rich diversity of ideas and methods of production, there is today a renewed vigour capable of raising British design to a new high level.

Demi-Gods or Boffins? The Designer's Image, 1936 to 1986

Fiona MacCarthy

In the latest volume of James Lees-Milne's diaries, beginning with the year 1948, there is a poignant portrait of the young Alex Moulton who comes to stay the night at his flat in Thurloe Square:

> He tells me he has invented a new steam-, paraffin-driven motor car and hopes to have the first model on the road this year. He is certain it will be a success, but says he can make no money out of it, such a thing these days being impossible. It is his means of creation ... We drank wine and talked till midnight.[1]

Lees-Milne is tremendously impressed with Alex Moulton: his earnestness, intelligence and, above all, his zeal.

In getting this exhibition together, a complex task involving examining the work of 130 élite British designers in very varied disciplines against the background of their attitudes and aims, I have become intensely aware of what unites them as well as what so obviously differentiates designers in some ways so disparate as Douglas Cockerell and Hardy Amies; or, to embark on even more unlikely pairings, Eric Gill and Lord Snowdon, Zandra Rhodes and Frank Whittle, Eileen Gray and Sir Barnes Wallis, Duncan Grant and Kenneth Grange. What unites them is, I think, this great quality of zealousness, the will to push forward, to extend the possibilities. It is becoming fashionable in certain jaundiced circles where the structuralist view of design history is favoured to argue that design is merely capitalist plotting. From this it follows the designer is a cynic. Possibly both he and she are now becoming a bit more so. But in the past half century it has not been the case.

The records of the Royal Designers for Industry bulge with the case histories of designers as idealists, designers as fanatics. The supreme example is Edward Gordon Craig, travelling the world in his black homburg and bow tie, the personification of passionate genius, intent on the vouchsafing of a vision and the exerting of an influence which, as Laurence Irving pointed out in his obituary, "had only limited practical expression".[2] But closer to home, and nearer feasibility, there are endless pictures of the design obsessionist. Cockerell, the bookbinder, faced with the technical problems of binding the *Codex Sinaiticus* for the British Museum, evolving a peculiar kind of linen for the purpose. Eileen Gray determinedly mastering the craft of lacquerwork, wild ambition for a lady in 1898. John Waterer, the suitcase and leatherwork designer, in reckless and successful pursuit of the zip-fastener. A. A. Rubbra working taciturnly through the war, upping the horsepower of the Merlin engine used in British fighter planes, a feat which had so drained him that once the war was over he had to take extended periods of rest. Colin Chapman flamboyantly developing the Lotus, at the very frontiers of knowledge, so to speak.

Before I go much further I must of course acknowledge my debt to Andrew Saint and his admirable study *The Image of the Architect*, one of the most original and brilliantly written books on architecture of the past few decades. His examination of the way that architects have interpreted their role, and also how that image has appeared to the outsider, has obviously influenced my own view of designers: inevitably so, since in their early years, from the middle thirties onwards when the first of the Royal Designers were appointed, industrial designers were very often architects, and architects right in the thick of that tradition which Andrew Saint describes as "the kindly, alluring, essentially harmless but increasing anachronistic concept of the architect as gentleman".[3] It was a romantic tradition, a well-meaning one, which led on to the Festival of Britain herbivores.

How did they see themselves, these gentleman designers? (Only one lady, the weaver Ethel Mairet, became an RDI in the years before the war). And how did they regard their relationship with industry? It is a very interesting question and easier to answer in those early days than later, when the European emigré faction was stronger. At the start the attitude was very English, almost jokey: design for industry was both a challenge and a game. "What ho!" wrote Eric Gill, one of the first of RDIs, when taken on by Monotype as their consultant in 1928. "This means advice in 'type faces'. Salary v. handsome too and I like typography don't you know".[4] A typically throw-away reaction. How much British design history in those two small words "What ho!".

These were the days before the organised design profession. The Society of Industrial Artists, founded in 1930, was only in its infancy when the Royal Society of Arts set up the Faculty. The title Royal Designers for Industry was established as more of a hope for the future than a precise statement of contemporary fact. For relationships between most early RDIs and industry were in actual practice rather ill-defined and random. For the generation up to and including Gordon Russell an industrial commission was a venture into unknown and slightly fearsome territory, brought to a conclusion with a sense of some relief. For an enchanting vision of designer as adventurer one has to look no further than the long obituary of Douglas Cockerell in the Royal Society of Arts *Journal*, by his colleague Noel Rooke. This consummate craftsman, ostensibly so reticent, the brother of Sir Sydney the Fitzwilliam director, controller of the Bindery at W. H. Smith, had had a most extraordinarily colourful life history beginning when, at the age of 15, he was removed from St. Paul's School by his mother and shipped away to Canada with steerage fare paid and only five pounds in his pocket. At a slightly later stage, in an even more unlikely episode, Cockerell became a manager with the Imperial Bank of Canada, "in charge of a branch in the Far West, in shirt sleeves, with a loaded revolver close to hand." Noel Rooke goes on to draw a parallel between these times of high adventure in the West and Cockerell's resilience in his later life as a designer:

His gaiety in facing difficulties must have been of great service to him in those early years; it never quite left him. He found that he liked cowboys very much indeed.[5]

The practice of design was seen in those days as, inevitably, a kind of confrontation. It was the legacy of the Arts and Crafts movement, steeped in the philosophy of Ruskin, to view design for industry as some sort of skirmish if not with capitalistic evils at least against the forces of visual apathy. The skill and the excitement lay in the outwitting of commercial opposition and seeing through into industrial production what it was felt (for these, in a sense, were rather condescending days) the public really wanted. The designer's role was pushing things, extending possibilities: as far as one could go; as much as they could take.

A noticeable trait in designers of this period is the element of *braggadocio*. By no means all of them were giant histrionic figures like Edward Gordon Craig, or Eric Gill eccentrics, or even recognisable Fine Artists, in the mould of Duncan Grant. Many were quite subdued in their manner and appearance. The early Royal Designers had a fairly large contingent of the gentlemanly letterers and printers, and the ethos of the Central School and W. R. Lethaby, that peculiar combination of modesty and bluffness, was prevalent throughout the thirties and the forties. Harold Stabler, elected in 1936 in the "Pottery, Enamelling and Silversmithing" category (I think the lone designer in this esoteric section), shared these characteristics, this English liking for the measured and the quiet and the cult of rurality. Summed up by Gordon Russell:

he had a wide knowledge and love of animals, especially birds, and of trees. He liked all country pursuits. I know few men who got so much pleasure from a day's walking on the Downs, making cider, pruning trees or even digging potatoes. He loved to sit in little country pubs and listen to dialect. He never forgot the old Westmorland gardener who told him he kept his paths straight without a line "by scowl o' brow and skew o' gob".[6]

In other words, Stabler cultivated a particularly English style of rural dullness. But as Russell points out, there was another side to Stabler, and this was his craving for ornament and show-off. Stabler, says Russell, "loved the word 'swagger' and would look at baroque carving for hours". He adds perceptively that if Stabler had had the good fortune to live in an age with a good carving tradition he would have done the loveliest work

One cannot help discovering a wonderful ambivalence in British design work of this period, partly so low-key, so deliberately boring, but at the same time so full of confidence and daring. The swagger element which was in fact so often present in the British design of the years around the war has rather been forgotten, obliterated first by Pevsnerian propaganda and subsequently by the common-sense pronouncements of the Council of Industrial Design. But the Faculty of Royal Designers recognised it. It was not taboo at all here in the heart of the establishment: clearly to be seen in the work of Francis Meynell, printer-typographer (elected 1945), and in the persona, a work of art itself, of the graphic designer Ashley Havinden, admitted to the Faculty in 1947. Gordon Russell himself was extremely keen on swagger, as well as on good cider, building walls and carving tombstones. One needs a certain sympathy with swagger to approach a comprehension of the British at design.

All designers, however convivial and clubbable, are by their very nature to some extent lone rangers. Francis Meynell, as well as delighting in experiments in the minutiae of arranging type on pages and disposing decoration – the exact width of a margin, the precise form of a fleuron – saw himself as an adventurer on fairly wide horizons, professionally, intellectually, politically. Wells Coates' very glamorous self-image was that of the architect-designer *sans frontières*: his stance was that of modern internationalist-rationalist. He wore a kimono to entertain in Knightsbridge. He was mad about the sea, an obsession he shared with many of the Royal Designers of that generation. Untrammeled lives, wide open spaces, new horizons: it suited their concept of creativity. The rugged Uffa Fox, the famous yachtsman, elected to the Faculty in the middle fifties in the official category of Small Boats Design, seemed more than the inventor of the modern racing dinghy.

He was in his day an almost perfect symbol of the adventurer-designer, determined and intransigent and something of a lady-killer.

The idea of the designer as intrepid hero figure, intent on making his own creative leap, on arriving somewhere nobody has been before, is nowhere better illustrated than in the autobiography of Geoffrey de Havilland, a book entitled so enticingly *Sky Fever*, in which the fiasco of the flight of his first plane, painstakingly constructed with his friend and partner Frank in a £50 workshop in the countryside in Hampshire in winter 1909, is winningly described in the language of the Biggles book:

I think it was a mixture of impatience and sheer will power that finally got the first de Havilland machine off on its first flight. And it was crass ignorance that caused it to come back again, violently and disastrously. The sudden stress was too much for the wings, which probably had a pretty fine margin of strength anyway. But I picked myself dizzily out of the wreckage . . .

We did not waste any time on regrets or prolonged farewells. We said goodbye to our kindly landlady but not a backward glance to the field and sheds. We would be back soon enough. A lorry was already on the way to collect the remnants of our first machine. At Fulham we could begin work at once. We felt no real sense of disappointment, for all the time we had been at Seven Barrows I think we had both thought subconsciously that our first trials would probably end in disaster. But this time, we knew, we would build an aeroplane that would fly.[7]

From the idea of the designer as adventurer it was only a short step to the autocrat designer. There are quite a number of autocratic figures in the annals of the Faculty: Sir William Lyons, the founder of Jaguar; Sir Barnes Wallis; Stanley Morison, the great typographer (who so resolutely, like the hero in the fairytale, refused a knighthood *thrice*). Though all of these paid lip-service to team work, and relied on it as the means of achieving their own creative aims, they were emphatically the decision makers: it was team work very much on their own terms.

There is very little sense of corporate effort in the early history of the RDIs. The legendary large-scale undertakings of the thirties in which so many Royal Designers were involved – design for the Orient Line and London Transport – were more an orchestration of individual talents than an exercise in working for a common cause. Interestingly enough, the most convinced account from these early years of the creative stimulus of being a designer at the very centre of a large industrial complex comes from Laurence Irving, whose career in the film industry first burgeoned in 1928 when Douglas Fairbanks invited him to Hollywood as Art Director on *The Man in the Iron Mask*, his last major silent picture. Irving's analysis of the skills required to balance the creative and the technical demands of film-making is based on a more modest view of the designer's function. He sees the designer as the catalyst.[8] This view of things came further into favour in the Festival period, more democratic years.

But before the Festival of course there was the War, a war which elicited from the designers, as from the whole nation, a considerable increase in co-operative spirit. To take just one obvious example, Uffa Fox used his experience in designing racing craft to design an airborne lifeboat which, parachuted down, saved the lives of hundreds of airmen shot down at sea. The drawing of this boat, which was made in plywood and designed to be unfolded automatically by the parachutes, is in Uffa Fox's Royal Society of Arts Archive, a tangible and, after all these years, a rather touching memory of designers' ingenuity in wartime.

It was a period in which the artist's ego was to some extent submerged in the service of the nation. In designing propaganda posters: "Your Talk May Kill Your Comrades"; "Rabbits Can Be Fed on . . ."; "Get in Shape for Civvy Street"; "Join the ATS". The war posters of Abram Games and Tom Eckersley have a particular power which Games attributed in retrospect to their "high purpose".[9] In designing Utility furnishings and fabrics, Gordon Russell, chairman of the Utility Furniture Design Panel, threw himself into this very complex task with an almost schoolboyish enthusiasm, seeing the potential for raising the whole standard of furniture for the mass of the people.[10] (A classically herbivorous ambition.) When the Board of Trade requested the members of the Incorporated Society of London Fashion Designers, including Hardy Amies, to submit a basic collection of Utility garments – a top-coat, a suit, an afternoon dress and a cotton overall dress – *Vogue* magazine made the patriotic comment that now "all women have the equal chance to buy beautifully designed clothes suitable to their lives and incomes. It is a revolutionary scheme and a heartening thought. It is, in fact, an outstanding example of applied democracy."[11]

A whole book, or at least a very lengthy chapter, could be written on the exploits of designers as official War Artists. The crossing of the Channel in the spring of 1940 by Edward Ardizzone, Edward Bawden and Barnett Freedman has in fact been evocatively described by Ardizzone in his book of war experiences *Baggage to the Enemy*.[12] These were all three very private idiosyncratic talents, but they were trained observers, with commercial experience, to some extent attuned to get the job done by the deadline. Their very personal records of public cataclysm are in a sense a triumph of designers' discipline. A similar professionalism can be seen in the transmutation of Anna Zinkeisen, the most feminine, romantic of pre-war commercial artists, into the meticulous recorder of the London blitz in all its gruesome detail. She produced a series of pathological and clinical drawings of wounds for the medical profession, drawings so accurate they almost seem surrealistic. Her hospital studies, such as those depicting first aid by candlelight in St. Mary's, Paddington, and Sir Archibald McIndoe, the plastic surgeon, operating in East Grinstead, are (as her *Times* obituary rightly put it) "in a particular *genre* of her own".[13]

But of all artistic war activities the one which was most suited to the talents and the personalities of Royal Designers at that period was the art of camouflage. It made use of their professional skills and patriotic urges and at the same time allowed licence to their very English liking for swagger and high spirits, for the folly and the jape. From 1941, for example, Robert Goodden worked on sea-going camouflage of naval ships and vessels and, being interested in the physiology of vision and in particular in a theory known as the Purkinje Effect, which concerns the difference in behaviour between one's day vision and night vision, persuaded the Director of Scientific Research that the answer to the problem of arriving at the colour least obvious to the enemy in all conditions lay in painting ships the strongest, purest blue colours obtainable. Bright blue ships materialized: designer's heaven![14] Hulme Chadwick was Chief Camouflage Officer for the Air Ministry, mainly involved in siting and camouflaging of a chain of radar stations to assist British fighters and bombers round the coastline. His widow recollects that he flew right round the edge of the British Isles on this assignment with two scientific boffins having hair-raising adventures, including being arrested as enemy spies.[15]

The exuberance, the Boys' Own spirit of the camouflagers, comes out well in an article written by Hugh Casson, himself an Air Force camouflage officer, in the *Architectural Review* in 1944. He suggests that subservient as designers tried to make themselves to the demands of war, which in this case meant concealment, the zest for personal expression would break out.

He admits that certain designers at that time even developed so personal a pattern style that those who were familiar with it could recognise at moderate range a camouflaged object as being the work of A or B. "This", as he comments, "may have been aesthetically amusing, but it was probably poor camouflage."

Hugh Casson found the camouflage idea irresistible, a piquant combination of the strange and the familiar. He was of course an architect, and after the rationalist rigours of the thirties in which he had been trained, followed by the austerities of wartime, the fantasies of camouflage – the licence for disguising one landscape as another, one building as another – seem to have struck him as a joy and a release:

> *For the architect a comparison with the playful and comic quality of eighteenth century rococo is irresistible. So many of the characteristics are the same – the use of optical illusion, the creation of fictitious movement in the structure, the carefully considered effects of light, the use of restless abstract ornament, the dynamic expression of the belief that the part has only value when it is considered as portion of the whole. The individual patterns too, which when combined create the whole composition, do not appear wholly unfamiliar to an eye which has grown accustomed to the abstract painting of the last thirty years.*[16]

He goes on to say that in the past few years camouflage has performed a useful war service, and to hope that its post-war contribution could be equally entertaining and no less valuable. In their way, these turned out to be prophetic words.

There was an intense romanticism in the period after the war, the bridging years from 1946 to the Festival of Britain, that almost isolated span of activity which, in this exhibition, I have called Post-war Revival. It was a hopeful period, yet shot through with a sense of melancholy and of strangeness, the balance of those opposites Hugh Casson had identified and loved in wartime. Book illustration in particular, the work of Edward Bawden, Lynton Lamb and Barnett Freedman, flourished in this rather twilight time, somewhere between war and peace.

This neo-romantic movement had a very private feeling. It was a view of England made more poignant and more curious by the privations of wartime: it verged on the surreal. One can see this in the way designers came back to the classics – Bawden illustrating Gulliver, for instance; Lamb beginning on his famous sequence of Oxford Classic bookjackets – with particular intensity, a kind of relief. Mixed with the personal vision was a sense of practicality, a mood of social realism,

strongly democratic and educational urges out of which emerged such well-meaning enterprises as the King Penguin series in its early post-war phase. King Penguin books were written by several Royal Designers. Royal Designers also illustrated the King Penguins. Indeed designers' outlook at that period is epitomised by that King Penguin series *The Things We See*.

Designers were beginning to regard themselves as less of lone performers, more as part of the whole social fabric. The *Britain Can Make It* exhibition got this over, and so did the exhibition which succeeded it, *Design At Work*, mounted by the RDIs at the Royal Academy in 1948. Design was becoming more serious and also in a sense much less flamboyant, more low key and less alarming. Milner Gray's RDI Address for 1955, given at the Royal Society of Arts, was wonderfully calming. He called it *The Creative Urge* and asked a basic question: what are the qualities of the ideal designer? First of all, "he" (the designer at this period is by definition male) must have the inward urge which brings new forms into being, every design being in a sense an act of communication, "a statement of a conviction about the nature and function of an article, for which the artist-designer assumes responsibility". Next – and this marks a considerable move in the shedding of self-consciousness about commerce – the designer's role includes assessing what will *sell*. Milner Gray maintains, with a humility unknown to the previous generation of designers, that the consumer, though he may be influenced by the ideas of designers, has his own standards of judgment. He cannot be coerced.[17]

The Festival of Britain, the third and much the largest of post-war design bonanzas, is now regarded mainly, down these vistas of nostalgia, as the start of a mass-public acceptance of the "modern" in design and architecture. This to some extent it was. But I think one has to see it in other ways as well. The Festival of Britain was also the beginning of a more democratic governmental policy towards design: *vide* Gordon Russell's guidelines to the Council of Industrial Design in 1950, when he was planning the Festival "Design Review". He says it is essential to aim at achieving a good standard of design which is broad in context, "not merely a personal preference which may degenerate into the taste of a small clique".[18]

Looking back at the Festival, there were some obvious individual design triumphs, such memorable objects as Ernest Race's "Antelope", the crystal-pattern fabrics, Robert Goodden's splendidly eccentric silver teaset for the Royal

Pavilion. But when it comes down to it the exhibition was a triumph less for individual designers than for co-ordination. The Festival of Britain opened up the possibilities inherent in designing and influenced the whole development of the modern multi-disciplinary design office.

The Festival was British, extravagantly so: the Lion and the Unicorn Pavilion was so British that looking at the photographs these days one almost cringes. But it is ironic that many of the main designers of the Festival, and indeed a high proportion of recruits to the Faculty of Royal Designers in the post-war period, had in fact arrived in Britain from abroad. Henrion, Schleger, Wolpe: all elected in 1959. Buzas, Groag, Leischner, Misha Black; Natasha Kroll; George Him, the topographer of Schweppshire; Hans Schmoller, famous Art Director of Penguin Books; Sir Alec Issigonis, born in Smyrna, the designer of the almost archetypal British car.

Where would British design have been without this foreign input? It is a pertinent question to consider in the midst of Royal Designers, at the heart of the establishment, where the middle-European accents still reverberate. It seems to me that British design, like English cooking, has in fact been enhanced greatly by a long tradition of foreign influence. British design these days is tolerant in outlook. Foreign influence has helped to preserve it from being hidebound, encouraging an elasticity and an intelligence which has given it so much of its staying power and strength.

As with any self-elected body, and especially a grouping aimed at furthering professional excellence, the ruling standards will repay a close analysis: the people they leave out (and why); the people they let in. In the last two decades the theoretic basis has changed considerably. The catchment is more catholic. There has been more emphasis on engineering, a re-balance not achieved without much heart-searching and argument; and at the other end of the spectrum a new appreciation of individualistic talent, a sense that excellence can also lie in the ephemeral and fashionable. Photography; and dress design; and television graphics. Royal Designers seem less solid than in 1936.

It is interesting that this rather evanescent quality, the individual flair which at its best approaches genius, far from being ironed out over the past half century, a period of great growth for the design profession, is valued now perhaps more than it ever has been. In one memorable year for RDI elections three women joined the Faculty, an episode I cite not just because it was so obviously a record, female Royal Designers being thinnish on the ground, but because it showed so clearly exactly what I mean about the way designers see themselves, the way they aim to balance the creative and the functional, individual expression with precise professionalism.

One of these designers was Eileen Gray, by then aged more than 90, a belated accolade but still a rather touching act of recognition to a high priestess of perfectionism, many of whose furniture designs continue in production, as visually valid today as in the twenties. One was Marianne Straub, a weaver who has broken down the barriers between handcraft and production, whose determination to be taken seriously as industrial designer, and as, indeed, a woman, at a period in which both these things were somewhat suspect in professional circles, has been very influential.

The third of the female designers, these Three Graces (as Francis Meynell, I am certain, would have christened them), was of course Jean Muir, a great designer of our time, whose whole approach, fastidiously practical, was immaculately summed up in an RDI Address *Clothes – Aesthetics – Design – Commerce*, in which she put across a designer's image of self-abnegation, a philosophy of almost unbelievable self-discipline. Is this in fact a dress designer speaking?

In making the pattern for any garment, system and accuracy is as important as in any engineering process; every measurement has to be exact to the millimetre, every line has to flow throughout, every grain has to be totally in balance. To me, the flat pattern is the most important part of the manufacturing of clothes. If the initial pattern is not correct, the size graded from it will not be correct. It has to be comprehensively exact for cutting and machining; every point to watch in making has to be listed to avoid any uncertainty. It is the blue print on which manufacturing sinks or swims.[19]

1. James Lees-Milne. *Midway on the Waves*. London, Faber, 1985.

2. Laurence Irving. Obit. Edward Gordon Craig. JRSA. October 1966.

3. Andrew Saint. *The Image of the Architect*. New Haven and London, Yale University Press, 1983.

4. Walter Shewring, ed. *Letters of Eric Gill*. London, Cape, 1947.

5. Noel Rooke. Obit. Douglas Cockerell. JRSA. Dec. 21, 1945.

6. Gordon Russell. Obit. Harold Stabler. JRSA. April 27, 1945.

7. Geoffrey de Havilland *Sky Fever*. London, Hamish Hamilton, 1961.

8. Laurence Irving. *The Affectation of Imperfection*, RDI Address reprinted in *Royal Designers On Design*. London, Design Council, 1986.

9. Quoted Zbynek Zeman. *Selling the War. Art and Propaganda in World War II*. London, Orbis, 1978.

10. Gordon Russell. *Designer's Trade*. London, George Allen & Unwin, 1968.

11. *Vogue* magazine, October 1942.

12. Edward Ardizzone. *Baggage to the Enemy*. London, John Murray, 1941.

13. Obit. Anna Zinkeisen. *The Times*, 25 September 1976.

14. Letter from Robert Goodden to the author, 13 May 1986.

15. Letter from Joy Chadwick to the author, 18 April 1986.

16. Hugh Casson. "The aesthetics of camouflage", article in *The Architectural Review*, September 1944.

17. Milner Gray. *The Creative Urge*, RDI Address reprinted in *Royal Designers on Design*. Ibid.

18. Gordon Russell. *Designer's Trade*. Ibid.

19. Jean Muir. *Clothes — Aesthetics – Design – Commerce*. JRSA. October, 1984.

Eileen Gray

E-1027 adjustable table with tubular steel frame, 1927. Originally designed for the E-1027 house at Roquebrune by Eileen Gray and Jean Badovici. After a long period of relative obscurity Eileen Gray's classic qualities as architect-designer were rediscovered and she was made an RDI in 1972 at the age of 93. This table was included in the collection of her furniture designs revived by Aram in the 1970s.
Aram Designs Ltd

Susie Cooper

Earthenware plate and covered vegetable dish Pattern 912, with "Crayon Lines" decoration, c.1935. Susie Cooper had set up her own factory in Tunstall in 1929 and specialised in hand-painted pottery, particularly banding, which from the mid-1930s she used in combination with lithographic patterns. The firm was a popular success in the middle market at that time, to such an extent that this design incorporates the designer's monogram.
Josiah Wedgwood & Son

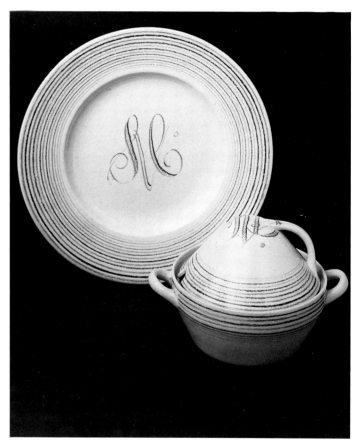

Charles Holden
Exterior of Arnos Grove Underground Station, 1933. One of the
famous series of stations designed by Holden for London Passenger
Transport Board under the aegis of Frank Pick. Arnos Grove was
singled out by Nikolaus Pevsner as "*perhaps more impeccably
satisfactory than any other*", on account of the way in which simplicity
of outline is combined with a remarkable delicacy of detail.
London Transport Museum

Christian Barman
Electric convector heater with chromed finish designed for HMV, 1934.
Victoria and Albert Museum

Robert Goodden
Ashtray from a series of low-cost mass-produced glass designs for Chance Brothers from 1934 onwards.
Morgan-Wells

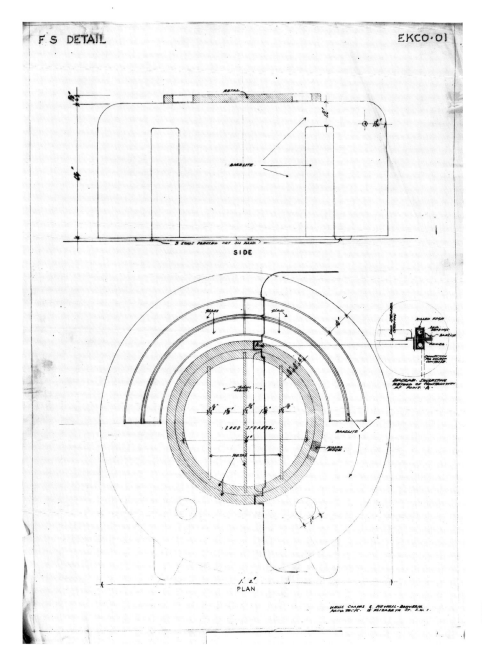

F S DETAIL   EKCO·01

SIDE

PLAN

Wells Coates
Design for Ecko wireless set AD65, 1934.
British Architectural Library/RIBA

Wells Coates
Ecko wireless set AD65, 1934. From 1932
Coates worked regularly for Ecko, who had
just built a large plastics moulding plant in
Southend. His designs were highly
innovative, with their moulded plastic
casing built around the circular
loudspeaker, and became a kind of status
symbol of their day, bearing out Coates'
comment of 1934: *"A radio set should never
be disguised as something else. It has its own
important function in the house and is in
many cases a possession regarded more as the
indoor equivalent of a car than a piece of
furniture."*
Victoria and Albert Museum

Anna Zinkeisen
''Dovercourt by Rail'' poster designed for LNER, 1935. Poster design was a remarkable example of public patronage of designers in the 1930s. Besides LNER, Southern Railways, London Passenger Transport Board and Shell Mex placed commissions regularly with such Royal Designers as Tom Purvis, Hans Schleger, Edward Bawden, Ashley Havinden and the Hon. RDI E. McKnight Kauffer.
Victoria and Albert Museum

Eric Gill
Gill "Sans Serif" type introduced by the Monotype Corporation in 1929. Gill Sans appears on the jackets of the first 10 Penguin books published in 1935 (as well as on the LNER poster shown opposite).

Berthold Wolpe
Broadsheet advertising "Albertus Capitals", a version of the typeface designed for the Monotype Corporation, 1936.

PENGUIN
BOOKS

THE BODLEY HEAD

ARIEL

ANDRÉ
MAUROIS

THE BODLEY HEAD

COMPLETE   UNABRIDGED

◆ ALBERTUS CAPITALS ◆

ABCDEFGHIJKLMNOPQ
CUT IN SEVEN SIZES
RSTUVWXYZ!?&MW&
FROM 14 TO 72 POINT
EXCLUSIVELY WITH
MONOTYPE· MACHINES

"MONOTYPE" SERIES 324

TRADE **MONOTYPE** MARK

LONDON
THE MONOTYPE CORPORATION LTD
43 & 44 FETTER LANE E.C.4

*. The word "Monotype" is the Registered Trade Mark of The Monotype Corporation Limited.   Registered Design No. 811437

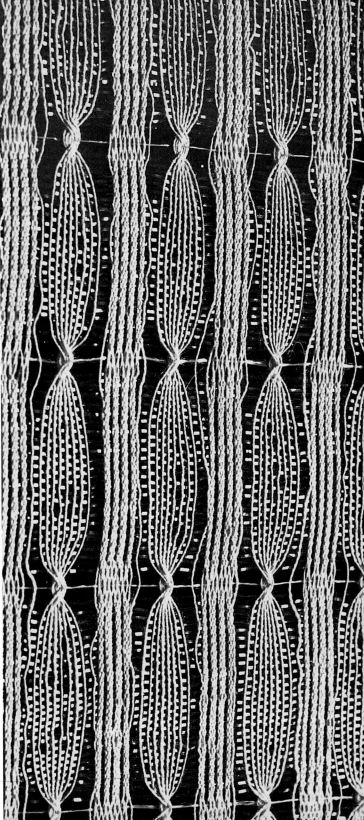

Duncan Grant

Design for "Apollo and Daphne" fabric, c.1933. One of a series of designs for screen-printed textiles produced by Grant in the mid-1930s for Allan Walton Textiles, some of which are currently being revived by Laura Ashley Ltd for inclusion in their 1987 collection. Allan Walton, a painter whose family owned a Manchester textiles firm, was himself an RDI.
Victoria and Albert Museum

Marianne Straub

Leno weave employing cellophane, designed for Helios, 1939. Marianne Straub joined Helios, then a new independent subsidiary of Barlow & Jones Ltd., in 1937. There she developed a range of woven and printed textiles with a high degree of design innovation, incorporating many novelty yarns as these became available to industry.
Warner & Sons Ltd

Enid Marx

Upholstery moquette designed for seating in London Passenger Transport Board trains, late 1930s. Enid Marx was one of a number of RDIs patronised by Frank Pick in the 1930s, and the tradition was continued by London Transport in the years after the war.

Frank Whittle

Whittle WU Jet Engine, 1937, rebuilt 1938. It was Whittle's inventive genius and brilliance in thermodynamic analysis which culminated in the first British jet flight in May 1941. He conceived a very simple design, appropriate to the technology of the time, which powered the Gloster E28/39 prototype aircraft, a project which, according to his RDI citation by Dr G.B.R. Feilden, *"must rank as one of the major technical achievements of the century"*.
Science Museum : Crown Copyright

William Lyons

SS 3½-litre Jaguar Saloon Car, 1936. The Swallow Sidecar Co., founded by William Lyons in 1922, had been floated as a public company in 1935. From then on, with the engineer William Heynes, Lyons continued to develop the SS range and – in the words of his RDI citation by Sir Francis Meynell – produced outstanding cars at remarkably low prices which won fame for this country throughout the world : *"He has not subjected himself to American trends : he has greatly influenced American trends. He has managed to penetrate what I may call 'the chromium curtain' of the United States. His car is a sine qua non for the heroes of American films, and in the words of Raymond Chandler a really smart and luxurious man-of-the-world is sure to have a Jaguar . . . Some cars, Sir, are made to look as if they are going very fast even when they are stock-still. That, I suppose, is an art. Other cars are made to look stable when they are going very, very fast. That is the better art of Mr. Lyons' Jaguar."*
The National Motor Museum, Beaulieu

Barnes Wallis
Interior of Vickers Wellington plane L4212.
Photograph taken in 1937 shows view
towards cockpit, with turret still to be fitted.
E. B. Morgan

Abram Games
"Your Talk May Kill Your Comrades",
1942. The best-known of a remarkable
series of posters commissioned by the
War Office, many carried out by RDIs.

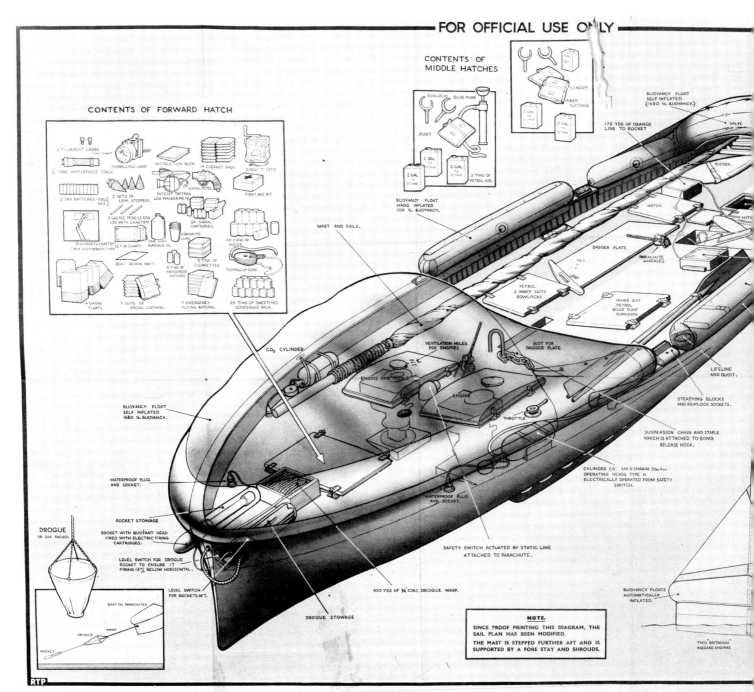

CONTENTS OF FORWARD HATCH

2 FILAMENT LAMPS.
ONE WATERPROOF TORCH.
12 DRY BATTERIES (S.W.2) NK 8.3
3 GREASE PENCILS FOR USE WITH CHARTBAG
BIGSWORTH CHARTBOARD C.W. 4 WATERPROOF COVER.
BOAT REPAIR MATS.
4 SMOKE FLOATS.
7 SUITS OF SPECIAL CLOTHING.
SIGNALLING LAMP
INSTRUCTION BOOK.
2 SETS OF LEAK STOPPERS.
PATENT TAFFRAIL LOG. WALKER MK IV.
SET OF CHARTS
3 TINS OF CIGARETTES
7 EMERGENCY FLYING RATIONS.
14 EVERHOT BAGS.
SIGNAL PISTOL
54 SIGNAL CARTRIDGES
ONE PINT MASSAGE OIL
3 DRINKING CUPS
3 TINS OF WATERPROOF MATCHES.
28 TINS OF SWEETENED CONDENSED MILK.
RADIO T.1333
FIRST AID KIT
44 CANS OF WATER.
TOPPING UP PUMP.

CONTENTS OF MIDDLE HATCHES

ROWLOCKS BILGE PUMP.
PORT
2 GAL. 73 OCTANE
2 GAL. 73 OCTANE
2 GAL. 73 OCTANE
STARB'D
INNER SUITINGS
2 GAL. 73 OCTANE
2 GAL. OIL
2 GAL. 73 OCTANE
3 TINS OF PETROL + OIL

BUOYANCY FLOAT HAND INFLATED 100 lb. BUOYANCY.

BUOYANCY FLOAT SELF INFLATED (1680 lb. BUOYANCY.)
175 YDS OF ORANGE LINE TO ROCKET
VALVE
RUDDER
HATCH.
DAGGER PLATE
PARACHUTE SHACKLES
PETROL 2 INNER SUITS ROWLOCKS
INNER SUIT PETROL BILGE PUMP ROWLOCKS

MAST AND SAILS.
CO2 CYLINDER
VENTILATION HOLES FOR ENGINES
SLOT FOR DAGGER PLATE
ENGINE AND TOOLS
ENGINE
THROTTLE
LIFELINE AND QUOIT.
STEADYING BLOCKS AND ROWLOCK SOCKETS.
SUSPENSION CHAIN AND STAPLE WHICH IS ATTACHED TO BOMB RELEASE HOOK.

BUOYANCY FLOAT SELF INFLATED 1680 lb. BUOYANCY.

WATERPROOF PLUG AND SOCKET.

ROCKET STOWAGE
ROCKET WITH BUOYANT HEAD FIRED WITH ELECTRIC FIRING CARTRIDGES.
LEVEL SWITCH FOR DROGUE ROCKET TO ENSURE IT FIRING 15% BELOW HORIZONTAL.

LEVEL SWITCH FOR ROCKETS AFT.

DROGUE STOWAGE

100 YDS OF 3/4 CIRC. DROGUE WARP.

WATERPROOF PLUG AND SOCKET.

CYLINDER CO. MK.II CHARGE 3 lbs. 4 oz. OPERATING HEADS TYPE H. ELECTRICALLY OPERATED FROM SAFETY SWITCH.

SAFETY SWITCH ACTUATED BY STATIC LINE ATTACHED TO PARACHUTE.

BUOYANCY FLOATS AUTOMATICALLY INFLATED.

TWO BRITANNIA INBOARD ENGINES

DROGUE OR SEA ANCHOR.

BOAT ON PARACHUTES.
DROGUE WARP
ROCKET.

NOTE.
SINCE PROOF PRINTING THIS DIAGRAM, THE SAIL PLAN HAS BEEN MODIFIED.
THE MAST IS STEPPED FURTHER AFT AND IS SUPPORTED BY A FORE STAY AND SHROUDS.

RTP

AIRBORNE LIFEBOAT Mk I - *Equipme*

PRINTED FOR H.M. STATIONERY OFFICE BY CHROMOWORKS LTD. LONDON. 51-3399.

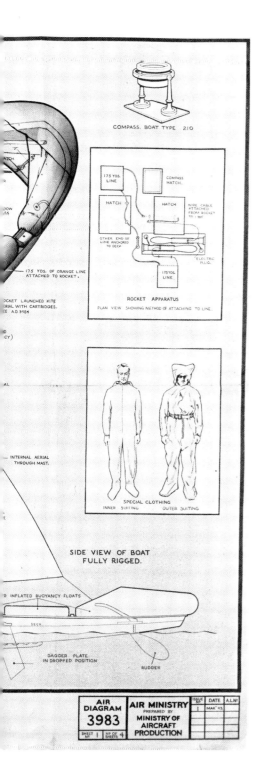

COMPASS, BOAT TYPE 210

175 YDS. LINE

COMPASS HATCH.

HATCH

HATCH

WIRE CABLE ATTACHED FROM ROCKET TO KITE

OTHER END OF LINE ANCHORED TO DECK

ELECTRIC PLUG.

175 YDS. LINE.

ROCKET APPARATUS

PLAN VIEW SHOWING METHOD OF ATTACHING TO LINE.

175 YDS. OF ORANGE LINE ATTACHED TO ROCKET.

ROCKET LAUNCHED KITE AERIAL WITH CARTRIDGES. SEE A.D. 3984

INTERNAL AERIAL THROUGH MAST.

SPECIAL CLOTHING
INNER SUITING   OUTER SUITING

SIDE VIEW OF BOAT FULLY RIGGED.

INFLATED BUOYANCY FLOATS

DECK

DAGGER PLATE IN DROPPED POSITION

RUDDER

AIR DIAGRAM 3983

AIR MINISTRY PREPARED BY MINISTRY OF AIRCRAFT PRODUCTION

SHEET Nº 1   Nº OF SHEETS 4

ISSUE Nº 1   DATE MAR 43   A.L.Nº

Uffa Fox

Diagram of equipment for the RAF Airborne Lifeboat Mk. 2, 1942. Fox already had an international reputation as a yacht designer at the outset of the war when he turned his talents to designing the parachuted airborne lifeboat which rescued hundreds of airmen shot down at sea. The 20-foot fold-up plywood boat, automatically unfolded by the parachutes, was self-righting and self-bailing, provided with food and clothing, and was designed to be motored, rowed or sailed to safety.
RDI Archive

Arthur Rubbra

Merlin Engine 60°V, 12 cylinder, supercharged aero engine. Rubbra worked on the design of the Merlin between 1939 and 1945. The engine powered 17 different operational aircraft during World War II, the most famous of which were the Hurricane, Spitfire, Lancaster, Mosquito and the American Mustang.
Rolls-Royce plc

Gordon Russell and Utility Furniture Advisory Committee
Utility living/dining room showing the original range of Utility
furniture, designed in 1942. The Board of Trade had set up the
Committee as a wartime measure under the Chairmanship of
Gordon Russell, and including Brian O'Rorke, another RDI, to
produce specifications for *"furniture of good, sound construction in
simple but agreeable designs for sale at reasonable prices, and ensuring
the maximum economy of raw materials and labour."* Gordon Russell
saw this as an opportunity to raise the whole national standard of
design.
Geffrye Museum: Inner London Education Authority

Roger Furse
Laurence Olivier in "Kingly Robes", costume designed for
Shakespeare's *Henry V*, 1944. Still from the film by courtesy of
The Rank Organisation plc.
National Film Archive, London

R. D. Russell
Murphy A146 wireless, 1948. Wireless in
mahogany veneer, made on the baffleboard
principle. One of the most successful
designs to develop from Dick Russell's long
collaboration with Murphy Radio Ltd
between 1931 and the late 1940s.
Victoria and Albert Museum

Robin Day
Hillestak chair in beech and preformed
plywood, designed in 1950. This was the
first low-cost mass-produced design to be
manufactured by Hille.
Photograph by John Rose and John Dyble

Hardy Amies/Edward Molyneux
"The New Look", 1949. Amies coat, left,
and Molyneux coat, right, photographed
inside the portico of the National Gallery.
Photograph by Norman Parkinson

Hugh Casson
Festival of Britain, South Bank Exhibition,
1951. View showing the Skylon from the
Fairway looking towards the Thames
with Dome of Discovery on the left.
Hugh Casson was Director of Architecture
for the Festival, co-ordinating
a large and complex exhibition scheme
which included contributions from many
RDIs and RDIs-to-be: Spence, Gardner,
Buzas, Henrion, Goodden, R. D. Russell,
Black, Gray, Marx, Straub, Ward and
others. The South Bank Exhibition also
featured "Design Review", a propaganda
collection of well-designed British
products assembled under the direction
of Gordon Russell, by this time Director
of the Council of Industrial Design.

Milner Gray
"Pyrex" oven-to-table glassware designed for J. A. Jobling Ltd.
1955. This was part of a large co-ordinated collection of casseroles,
roasting dishes, serving bowls, launched with a new Pyrex
trademark also designed by Gray. Like David Mellor's "Pride"
cutlery, shown opposite, it was included in the first Design Centre
Awards in 1957.
Photograph John Maltby Ltd

Robert Welch
Nutcrackers in stainless steel designed for Old Hall, 1958. Welch was design consultant to Old Hall from 1955, producing a range of tableware which soon began to challenge the Swedish pre-eminence in design of modern stainless steel.
Design Council

David Mellor
"Pride" cutlery in silver plate with white xylonite knife handle, 1954. Originally designed for Walker & Hall Ltd and still in production by David Mellor, Sheffield.
Photograph Pete Hill

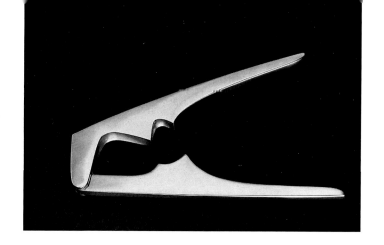

Mary Quant
Bazaar, Mary Quant's first boutique,
opened in King's Road in 1955, and its
youthful zany style was to become
established as the epitome of Swinging
Sixties London.
Photograph: David Bailey

Alec Issigonis
Morris Mini motor-car, sketch design in
early stages, 1959.
The National Motor Museum, Beaulieu

Alec Issigonis
Morris Minor 1000, 4-door saloon version,
1962/3, of car which first went into
production in 1948. At that date its
engineering was extremely innovative and
it stayed in production for over 20 years.
The National Motor Museum, Beaulieu

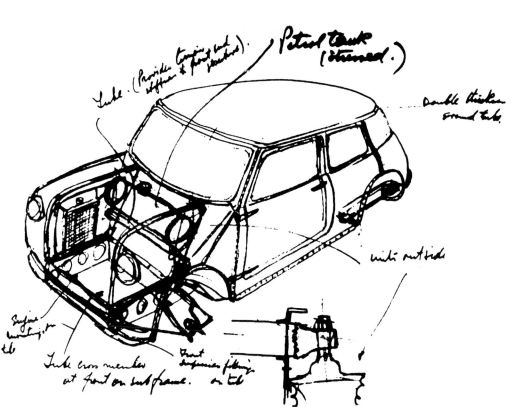

Lionel Haworth
Viscount aircraft, angled view showing the Dart engine, powerplant
of which was designed by Lionel Haworth, 1945 to 1963.
Rolls-Royce plc

James Gardner
QEII liner for Cunard, 1962. Gardner was responsible for the above-
water lines of the ship, with a team of designers, including other
RDIs, being allotted sections of the interior. Like Basil Spence's
Coventry Cathedral, this project harked back to the Festival of
Britain principle of collaborative modern design.

Lionel Haworth
Concorde aircraft, angled view showing the Olympus engines,
powerplants of which were designed by Lionel Haworth,
1964 to 1977.
Rolls-Royce plc

Ian Proctor
22-foot International Tempest Class Yacht,
1966. Proctor's Tempest Class Yachts were
selected for use in the 1968 and 1972
Olympics.
Eileen Ramsay

W. C. Brown

Bosphorus Bridge, Istanbul, Turkey, designed 1970 to 1973.
This bridge by Dr Brown, also the designer of bridges across the
Volta River, Severn and Wye and Humber, provides the only direct
route between Asia and Europe south of the Black Sea. In an
illuminating address to the Royal Society of Arts in 1982, entitled
Strength through Shape, Dr Brown put forward his view that while
RDIs are all individualists they have one great common link which
is that they are all *"struggling to create something for others to* use".
He went on to cite designers' common experience that even when
they seem to be succeeding most they are always brought back again
face to face with *"that greatest leveller of all, the plain sheet of paper
on the drawing board"*.
Turkish Tourist Office

Natasha Kroll
Set design for *Eugene Onegin* for BBC TV, 1967.

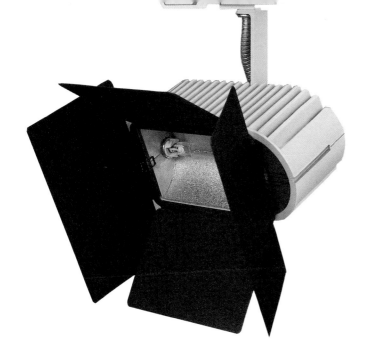

Robert Heritage
"Powerflood" light fitting designed for Concorde Lighting, 1969. A high-intensity floodlight used in theatres, workshops, shops, etc. The body is heavily finned to help dissipate the large output of heat. The design received a Council of Industrial Design Award in 1971 and the Bundespreis Gute Form in 1972.
Concorde Lighting Ltd

David Gentleman
Stamps from four different sets designed for the Post Office between 1972 and 1984. David Gentleman has been the most prolific designer of postage stamps over the past two decades. His first stamps were issued in 1962 and in 1965, at the time when Anthony Wedgwood Benn was Postmaster-General, the Post Office commissioned *The Gentleman Album*, exploring the graphic possibilities of a more coherent stamp-issuing policy.

Bernard Lodge
Stills from the title sequence to *Dr Who* for BBC TV, 1973. Version 2 won the D & AD Silver Award in 1968; Version 4 won the Pye TV Award in 1973.

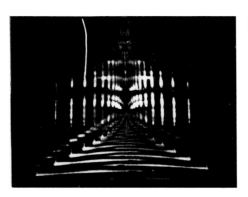

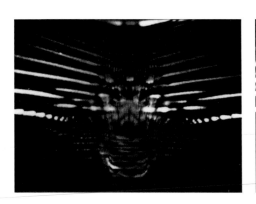

BBC 1922/1972

3P

BBC 1922/1972

5P

BBC 1922/1972

7½P

Social Reformers   Robert Owen

10P

Social Reformers

Lord Shaftesbury

11P

Social Reformers   Elizabeth Fry

13P

Prizewinning fire engine 1863

5½P

Fire engine 1766

10P

First steam fire engine 1830

8P

THE TWELVE DAYS OF CHRISTMAS

7P

THE TWELVE DAYS OF CHRISTMAS

9P

THE TWELVE DAYS OF CHRISTMAS

7P

F. H. K. Henrion
Symbol for the National Theatre, 1975.

Matthew Carter
Specimen settings for the New York Telephone Directory designed by Matthew Carter in 1978. This uses Carter's own Bell Centennial type specially developed for high-speed CRT typesetting.

Herbert Spencer
The Visible Word: problems of legibility, 1969. Book written and designed by Herbert Spencer following his appointment as Senior Research Fellow at the Royal College of Art to conduct a programme of research into the legibility of print in information publishing. He was subsequently Professor of Graphic Arts at the RCA from 1978 to 1984.

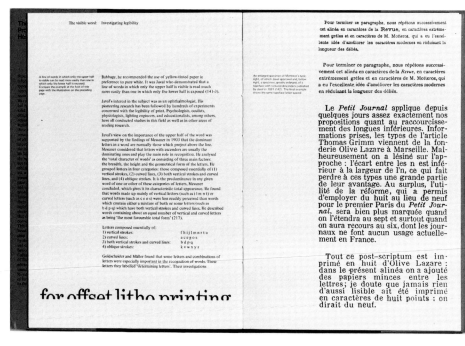

2:4:5

Blumberg A 24 BluespruceLn 473-0926
Blumberg Herman 332 E 14 581-5916
Blumberg Leroy 13 Adams EIslip 567-1278
Blumberg T E 4 Leeds Hntgtn 549-1487
Blumen Louis atty
51 Hawthorn HamptonBays 864-3597
Blumenfeld Irving 254 Amity 589-4774
Blumenthal Ernest 1135 Bensn 420-1581
Blumenthal O I 2424 3Av 477-1098
Blundell Thos 335 BrghtnBchAv LA 7-5264
Blunt Alison A 5 Hancock 698-5118
Blunt Edw 212 AllenHwy OystrBay TA 4-7143
Blunt Heather 3344 Orchard 757-6584
Blunt H T 12 AvenueL 589-3609
Bly E 513 32 283-0441
Boccio Angelo 24 Bayard 884-7204
BOCHIETTO SELHAM SCHOOL
44 Indpndnce Blvd 580-0432
Bock Alexander
55 OldTownLine Amtyvl 213-0652
Bock Harry O 1454 Isham 229-1637
Bodine Lawrence 3 HeathLane 662-7504
Bodkin Trudy 2113 Elmont 698-6057
Bodkin Thomas 414 EdmuntonTrnpk 281-1818
Boeckmann Henry 252 E 14 694-2248
Boehme Elizabeth 1133 2Av 765-5570
Boilermakers Local 5 42 Lynbrk 234-3751
Bojuk Lowell foreign change broker
234 Tulip 567-2598
Bolden Buddy 311 AvenueL 423-2923
Bolger Abraham 425 ElmwdAv 472-2186
Bolger H 2314 Albrmrle LngBch 924-3346
Boll Emma 3 Hillsboro 427-5162
Bolt Electric 1345 AvenueAmericas 242-3473
Bolt Harriet E 522 Bergen 277-0116
Bombara Oscar
241 Hicksville Bthpg HA 3-6850
Bomhoff Lena 3241 Brghtn 13 261-9399
Bonadonna Alphonso 331 E 44 437-2438
Bonanza L A 5411 AvenueB 549-1486
Bonanza Theodore
22 HollandTrnpk 259-8849
Bonaventura Orfeo
3 LngBch Ocnsid OH 9-6094
Bon-Bon Enterprises Inc
154 Logan 586-2061
Bond Edmund 5355 Bayard 585-1589
Bond Edw 123 E 2 226-7717
Bond Horst 21 EllsworthAv Lndnhrst 226-0623
Boone Emmett 44 Orchard 12 473-1908
Boone Hazel frt bskts 213 Henry 587-3605
BOOT SALES 213 52 838-9696
Bounds Travel Agency Inc
452 BennettLn 273-3720
Bourguignon International Inc
3 E 32 598-3720
Boxleyheath Opthalmics 5123 Hooper
Employment Ofc 853-6175
Immediate Treatment 853-8002
Information 853-9271
Bradley Industries Inc
325 EvrgrnAv 573-2391
Bradley Lennie HilltopHwy Bohmia 293-9186
Bradley Otis 115 BklynAv 289-5237
Bramble Ellsworth 4355 Loring 667-2863
Bramble Lorna Theresa
TownHse4 EIslip 583-5534
Brandt Thaddeus 231 Trnty 234-2380
Brassell A 4 HornLn Lynbrk 654-1287
Brassell Elsie 1125 5Av 269-9451
Brassell Thos O
534 TaylrAv Bethpge 884-8925
Breguet Henri 14 HemlockLn Brkhvn 273-7446
Brendon L 4223 EdgcmbAv 367-3275
Brennan Anna 15 Arbor 242-3098
Brice Herbert 25 Bldwn Hmnstd 281-3222
Brice T Edgar 5412 Hyman LT 9-4704
Briscoe Barbara 4 Hancock LngBch HA 3-8984
British European Airways
1523 E 54 878-1571
Britt Ollie 3 HooverBlvd 549-4555
Britt T 455 AvenueA 751-4350
Brittingham H 1221 Logan 226-5225
Broadway Lumber 2134 Bergen 694-1901
Bway Theatr 412 Bway 957-8086
Brock Louis 123 E 45 957-1752
Brock Oran 3115 Oakwd EHmptn 286-8638
Brockington Isiah 212 32 864-1173
Broder H 1144 Barbra 543-2847
Broderick Edw 31 TheBeeches 588-9419
Brodsky Edith 2 HeathLn Babyln 979-0893
Bronco Lounge 514 EBway Amtyvl 724-3208
Brook Lester bldr 423 4Av 543-7755
Bronx Boiler Inc 521 TurfLn 665-0982
Bklyn Academy 3244 EdwardsBlvd 924-6618
Bklyn Baptist Tabernacle
413 AvenueH 583-5530
Brooklyn Tavern Owners Assoc Inc

2:3:5 GROT

Blumberg A 24 BluespruceLn 473-0926
Blumberg Herman 332 E 14 581-5916
Blumberg Leroy 13 Adams EIslip 567-1278
Blumberg T E 4 Leeds Hntgtn 549-1487
Blumen Louis atty
51 Hawthorn HamptonBays 864-3597
Blumenfeld Irving 254 Amity 589-4774
Blumenthal Ernest 1135 Bensn 420-1581
Blumenthal O I 2424 3Av 477-1098
Blundell Thos 335 BrghtnBchAv LA 7-5264
Blunt Alison A 5 Hancock 698-5118
Blunt Edw 212 AllenHwy OystrBay TA 4-7143
Blunt Heather 3344 Orchard 757-6584
Blunt H T 12 AvenueL 589-3609
Bly E 513 32 283-0441
Boccio Angelo 24 Bayard 884-7204
BOCHIETTO SELHAM SCHOOL
44 Indpndnce Blvd 580-0432
Bock Alexander
55 OldTownLine Amtyvl 213-0652
Bock Harry O 1454 Isham 229-1637
Bodine Lawrence 3 HeathLane 662-7504
Bodkin Trudy 2113 Elmont 698-6057
Bodkin Thomas
414 EdmuntonTrnpk 281-1818
Boeckmann Henry 252 E 14 694-2248
Boehme Elizabeth 1133 2Av 765-5570
Boilermakers Local 5 42 Lynbrk 234-3751
Bojuk Lowell foreign change broker
234 Tulip 567-2598
Bolden Buddy 311 AvenueL 423-2923
Bolger Abraham 425 ElmwdAv 472-2186
Bolger H 2314 Albrmrle LngBch 924-3346
Boll Emma 3 Hillsboro 427-5162
Bolt Electric
1345 AvenueAmericas 242-3473
Bolt Harriet E 522 Bergen 277-0116
Bombara Oscar
241 Hicksville Bthpg HA 3-6850
Bomhoff Lena 3241 Brghtn 13 261-9399
Bonadonna Alphonso 331 E 44 437-2438
Bonanza L A 5411 AvenueB 549-1486
Bonanza Theodore
22 HollandTrnpk 259-8849
Bonaventura Orfeo
3 LngBch Ocnsid OH 9-6094
Bon-Bon Enterprises Inc
154 Logan 586-2061
Bond Edmund 5355 Bayard 585-1589
Bond Edw 123 E 2 226-7717
Bond Horst
21 EllsworthAv Lndnhrst 226-0623
Boone Emmett 44 Orchard 12 473-1908
Boone Hazel frt bskts 213 Henry 587-3605
BOOT SALES 213 52 838-9696
Bounds Travel Agency Inc
452 BennettLn 273-3720
Bourguignon International Inc
3 E 32 598-3720
Boxleyheath Opthalmics 5123 Hooper
Employment Ofc 853-6175
Immediate Treatment 853-8002
Information 853-9271
Bradley Industries Inc
325 EvrgrnAv 573-2391
Bradley Lennie
HilltopHwy Bohmia 293-9186
Bradley Otis 115 BklynAv 289-5237
Bramble Ellsworth 4355 Loring 667-2863
Bramble Lorna Theresa
TownHse4 EIslip 583-5534
Brandt Thaddeus 231 Trnty 234-2380
Brassell A 4 HornLn Lynbrk 654-1287
Brassell Elsie 1125 5Av 269-9451
Brassell Thos O
534 TaylrAv Bethpge 884-8925
Breguet Henri
14 HemlockLn Brkhvn 273-7446
Brendon L 4223 EdgcmbAv 367-3275
Brennan Anna 15 Arbor 242-3098
Brice Herbert 25 Bldwn Hmnstd 281-3222
Brice T Edgar 5412 Hyman LT 9-4704
Briscoe Barbara
4 Hancock LngBch HA 3-8984
British European Airways
1523 E 54 878-1571
Britt Ollie 3 HooverBlvd 549-4555
Britt T 455 AvenueA 751-4350
Brittingham H 1221 Logan 226-5225
Broadway Lumber 2134 Bergen 694-1901
Bway Theatr 412 Bway 957-8086
Brock Louis 123 E 45 957-1752
Brock Oran 3115 Oakwd EHmptn 286-8638
Brockington Isiah 212 32 864-1173
Broder H 1144 Barbra 543-2847
Broderick Edw 31 TheBeeches 588-9419
Brodsky Edith 2 HeathLn Babyln 979-0893
Bronco Lounge

1:4:5 GROT

Blumberg A 24 BluespruceLn 473-0926
Blumberg Herman 332 E 14 581-5916
Blumberg Leroy 13 Adams EIslip 567-1278
Blumberg T E 4 Leeds Hntgtn 549-1487
Blumen Louis atty
51 Hawthorn HamptonBays 864-3597
Blumenfeld Irving 254 Amity 589-4774
Blumenthal Ernest 1135 Bensn 420-1581
Blumenthal O I 2424 3Av 477-1098
Blundell Thos 335 BrghtnBchAv LA 7-5264
Blunt Alison A 5 Hancock 698-5118
Blunt Edw 212 AllenHwy OystrBay TA 4-7143
Blunt Heather 3344 Orchard 757-6584
Blunt H T 12 AvenueL 589-3609
Bly E 513 32 283-0441
Boccio Angelo 24 Bayard 884-7204
BOCHIETTO SELHAM SCHOOL
44 Indpndnce Blvd 580-0432
Bock Alexander
55 OldTownLine Amtyvl 213-0652
Bock Harry O 1454 Isham 229-1637
Bodine Lawrence 3 HeathLane 662-7504
Bodkin Trudy 2113 Elmont 698-6057
Bodkin Thomas 414 EdmuntonTrnpk 281-1818
Boeckmann Henry 252 E 14 694-2248
Boehme Elizabeth 1133 2Av 765-5570
Boilermakers Local 5 42 Lynbrk 234-3751
Bojuk Lowell foreign change broker
234 Tulip 567-2598
Bolden Buddy 311 AvenueL 423-2923
Bolger Abraham 425 ElmwdAv 472-2186
Bolger H 2314 Albrmrle LngBch 924-3346
Boll Emma 3 Hillsboro 427-5162
Bolt Electric 1345 AvenueAmericas 242-3473
Bolt Harriet E 522 Bergen 277-0116
Bombara Oscar
241 Hicksville Bthpg HA 3-6850
Bomhoff Lena 3241 Brghtn 13 261-9399
Bonadonna Alphonso 331 E 44 437-2438
Bonanza L A 5411 AvenueB 549-1486
Bonanza Theodore
22 HollandTrnpk 259-8849
Bonaventura Orfeo
3 LngBch Ocnsid OH 9-6094
Bon-Bon Enterprises Inc
154 Logan 586-2061
Bond Edmund 5355 Bayard 585-1589
Bond Edw 123 E 2 226-7717
Bond Horst 21 EllsworthAv Lndnhrst 226-0623
Boone Emmett 44 Orchard 12 473-1908
Boone Hazel frt bskts 213 Henry 587-3605
BOOT SALES 213 52 838-9696
Bounds Travel Agency Inc
452 BennettLn 273-3720
Bourguignon International Inc
3 E 32 598-3720
Boxleyheath Opthalmics 5123 Hooper
Employment Ofc 853-6175
Immediate Treatment 853-8002
Information 853-9271
Bradley Industries Inc
325 EvrgrnAv 573-2391
Bradley Lennie HilltopHwy Bohmia 293-9186
Bradley Otis 115 BklynAv 289-5237
Bramble Ellsworth 4355 Loring 667-2863
Bramble Lorna Theresa
TownHse4 EIslip 583-5534
Brandt Thaddeus 231 Trnty 234-2380
Brassell A 4 HornLn Lynbrk 654-1287
Brassell Elsie 1125 5Av 269-9451
Brassell Thos O
534 TaylrAv Bethpge 884-8925
Breguet Henri 14 HemlockLn Brkhvn 273-7446
Brendon L 4223 EdgcmbAv 367-3275
Brennan Anna 15 Arbor 242-3098
Brice Herbert 25 Bldwn Hmnstd 281-3222
Brice T Edgar 5412 Hyman LT 9-4704
Briscoe Barbara 4 Hancock LngBch HA 3-8984
British European Airways
1523 E 54 878-1571
Britt Ollie 3 HooverBlvd 549-4555
Britt T 455 AvenueA 751-4350
Brittingham H 1221 Logan 226-5225
Broadway Lumber 2134 Bergen 694-1901
Bway Theatr 412 Bway 957-8086
Brock Louis 123 E 45 957-1752
Brock Oran 3115 Oakwd EHmptn 286-8638
Brockington Isiah 212 32 864-1173
Broder H 1144 Barbra 543-2847
Broderick Edw 31 TheBeeches 588-9419
Brodsky Edith 2 HeathLn Babyln 979-0893
Bronco Lounge 514 EBway Amtyvl 724-3208
Brook Lester bldr 423 4Av 543-7755
Bronx Boiler Inc 521 TurfLn 665-0982
Bklyn Academy 3244 EdwardsBlvd 924-6618
Bklyn Baptist Tabernacle
413 AvenueH 583-5530
Brooklyn Tavern Owners Assoc Inc

1:3:5

Blumberg A 24 BluespruceLn 473-0926
Blumberg Herman 332 E 14 581-5916
Blumberg Leroy 13 Adams EIslip 567-1278
Blumberg T E 4 Leeds Hntgtn 549-1487
Blumen Louis atty
51 Hawthorn HamptonBays 864-3597
Blumenfeld Irving 254 Amity 589-4774
Blumenthal Ernest 1135 Bensn 420-1581
Blumenthal O I 2424 3Av 477-1098
Blundell Thos 335 BrghtnBchAv LA 7-5264
Blunt Alison A 5 Hancock 698-5118
Blunt Edw 212 AllenHwy OystrBay TA 4-7143
Blunt Heather 3344 Orchard 757-6584
Blunt H T 12 AvenueL 589-3609
Bly E 513 32 283-0441
Boccio Angelo 24 Bayard 884-7204
BOCHIETTO SELHAM SCHOOL
44 Indpndnce Blvd 580-0432
Bock Alexander
55 OldTownLine Amtyvl 213-0652
Bock Harry O 1454 Isham 229-1637
Bodine Lawrence 3 HeathLane 662-7504
Bodkin Trudy 2113 Elmont 698-6057
Bodkin Thomas
414 EdmuntonTrnpk 281-1818
Boeckmann Henry 252 E 14 694-2248
Boehme Elizabeth 1133 2Av 765-5570
Boilermakers Local 5 42 Lynbrk 234-3751
Bojuk Lowell foreign change broker
234 Tulip 567-2598
Bolden Buddy 311 AvenueL 423-2923
Bolger Abraham 425 ElmwdAv 472-2186
Bolger H 2314 Albrmrle LngBch 924-3346
Boll Emma 3 Hillsboro 427-5162
Bolt Electric
1345 AvenueAmericas 242-3473
Bolt Harriet E 522 Bergen 277-0116
Bombara Oscar
241 Hicksville Bthpg HA 3-6850
Bomhoff Lena 3241 Brghtn 13 261-9399
Bonadonna Alphonso 331 E 44 437-2438
Bonanza L A 5411 AvenueB 549-1486
Bonanza Theodore
22 HollandTrnpk 259-8849
Bonaventura Orfeo
3 LngBch Ocnsid OH 9-6094
Bon-Bon Enterprises Inc
154 Logan 586-2061
Bond Edmund 5355 Bayard 585-1589
Bond Edw 123 E 2 226-7717
Bond Horst
21 EllsworthAv Lndnhrst 226-0623
Boone Emmett 44 Orchard 12 473-1908
Boone Hazel frt bskts 213 Henry 587-3605
BOOT SALES 213 52 838-9696
Bounds Travel Agency Inc
452 BennettLn 273-3720
Bourguignon International Inc
3 E 32 598-3720
Boxleyheath Opthalmics 5123 Hooper
Employment Ofc 853-6175
Immediate Treatment 853-8002
Information 853-9271
Bradley Industries Inc
325 EvrgrnAv 573-2391
Bradley Lennie
HilltopHwy Bohmia 293-9186
Bradley Otis 115 BklynAv 289-5237
Bramble Ellsworth 4355 Loring 667-2863
Bramble Lorna Theresa
TownHse4 EIslip 583-5534
Brandt Thaddeus 231 Trnty 234-2380
Brassell A 4 HornLn Lynbrk 654-1287
Brassell Elsie 1125 5Av 269-9451
Brassell Thos O
534 TaylrAv Bethpge 884-8925
Breguet Henri
14 HemlockLn Brkhvn 273-7446
Brendon L 4223 EdgcmbAv 367-3275
Brennan Anna 15 Arbor 242-3098
Brice Herbert 25 Bldwn Hmnstd 281-3222
Brice T Edgar 5412 Hyman LT 9-4704
Briscoe Barbara
4 Hancock LngBch HA 3-8984
British European Airways
1523 E 54 878-1571
Britt Ollie 3 HooverBlvd 549-4555
Britt T 455 AvenueA 751-4350
Brittingham H 1221 Logan 226-5225
Broadway Lumber 2134 Bergen 694-1901
Bway Theatr 412 Bway 957-8086
Brock Louis 123 E 45 957-1752
Brock Oran 3115 Oakwd EHmptn 286-8638
Brockington Isiah 212 32 864-1173
Broder H 1144 Barbra 543-2847
Broderick Edw 31 TheBeeches 588-9419
Brodsky Edith 2 HeathLn Babyln 979-0893
Bronco Lounge

2:4:5

Blumberg A 24 BluespruceLn 473-0926
Blumberg Herman 332 E 14 581-5916
Blumberg Leroy 13 Adams EIslip 567-1278
Blumberg T E 4 Leeds Hntgtn 549-1487
Blumen Louis atty
51 Hawthorn HamptonBays 864-3597
Blumenfeld Irving 254 Amity 589-4774
Blumenthal Ernest 1135 Bensn 420-1581
Blumenthal O I 2424 3Av 477-1098
Blundell Thos 335 BrghtnBchAv LA 7-5264
Blunt Alison A 5 Hancock 698-5118
Blunt Edw 212 AllenHwy OystrBay TA 4-7143
Blunt Heather 3344 Orchard 757-6584
Blunt H T 12 AvenueL 589-3609
Bly E 513 32 283-0441
Boccio Angelo 24 Bayard 884-7204
BOCHIETTO SELHAM SCHOOL
44 Indpndnce Blvd 580-0432
Bock Alexander
55 OldTownLine Amtyvl 213-0652
Bock Harry O 1454 Isham 229-1637
Bodine Lawrence 3 HeathLane 662-7504
Bodkin Trudy 2113 Elmont 698-6057
Bodkin Thomas 414 EdmuntonTrnpk 281-1818
Boeckmann Henry 252 E 14 694-2248
Boehme Elizabeth 1133 2Av 765-5570
Boilermakers Local 5 42 Lynbrk 234-3751
Bojuk Lowell foreign change broker
234 Tulip 567-2598
Bolden Buddy 311 AvenueL 423-2923
Bolger Abraham 425 ElmwdAv 472-2186
Bolger H 2314 Albrmrle LngBch 924-3346
Boll Emma 3 Hillsboro 427-5162
Bolt Electric 1345 AvenueAmericas 242-3473
Bolt Harriet E 522 Bergen 277-0116
Bombara Oscar
241 Hicksville Bthpg HA 3-6850
Bomhoff Lena 3241 Brghtn 13 261-9399
Bonadonna Alphonso 331 E 44 437-2438
Bonanza L A 5411 AvenueB 549-1486
Bonanza Theodore
22 HollandTrnpk 259-8849
Bonaventura Orfeo
3 LngBch Ocnsid OH 9-6094
Bon-Bon Enterprises Inc
154 Logan 586-2061
Bond Edmund 5355 Bayard 585-1589
Bond Edw 123 E 2 226-7717
Bond Horst 21 EllsworthAv Lndnhrst 226-0623
Boone Emmett 44 Orchard 12 473-1908
Boone Hazel frt bskts 213 Henry 587-3605
BOOT SALES 213 52 838-9696
Bounds Travel Agency Inc
452 BennettLn 273-3720
Bourguignon International Inc
3 E 32 598-3720
Boxleyheath Opthalmics 5123 Hooper
Employment Ofc 853-6175
Immediate Treatment 853-8002
Information 853-9271
Bradley Industries Inc
325 EvrgrnAv 573-2391
Bradley Lennie HilltopHwy Bohmia 293-9186
Bradley Otis 115 BklynAv 289-5237
Bramble Ellsworth 4355 Loring 667-2863
Bramble Lorna Theresa
TownHse4 EIslip 583-5534
Brandt Thaddeus 231 Trnty 234-2380
Brassell A 4 HornLn Lynbrk 654-1287
Brassell Elsie 1125 5Av 269-9451
Brassell Thos O
534 TaylrAv Bethpge 884-8925
Breguet Henri 14 HemlockLn Brkhvn 273-7446
Brendon L 4223 EdgcmbAv 367-3275
Brennan Anna 15 Arbor 242-3098
Brice Herbert 25 Bldwn Hmnstd 281-3222
Brice T Edgar 5412 Hyman LT 9-4704
Briscoe Barbara 4 Hancock LngBch HA 3-8984
British European Airways
1523 E 54 878-1571
Britt Ollie 3 HooverBlvd 549-4555
Britt T 455 AvenueA 751-4350
Brittingham H 1221 Logan 226-5225
Broadway Lumber 2134 Bergen 694-1901
Bway Theatr 412 Bway 957-8086
Brock Louis 123 E 45 957-1752
Brock Oran 3115 Oakwd EHmptn 286-8638
Brockington Isiah 212 32 864-1173
Broder H 1144 Barbra 543-2847
Broderick Edw 31 TheBeeches 588-9419
Brodsky Edith 2 HeathLn Babyln 979-0893
Bronco Lounge 514 EBway Amtyvl 724-3208
Brook Lester bldr 423 4Av 543-7755
Bronx Boiler Inc 521 TurfLn 665-0982
Bklyn Academy 3244 EdwardsBlvd 924-6618
Bklyn Baptist Tabernacle
413 AvenueH 583-5530
Brooklyn Tavern Owners Assoc Inc

George Mackie
Bookjacket for *Catacomb Suburb*, poems by Alastair Fowler,
published by Edinburgh University Press, 1976.

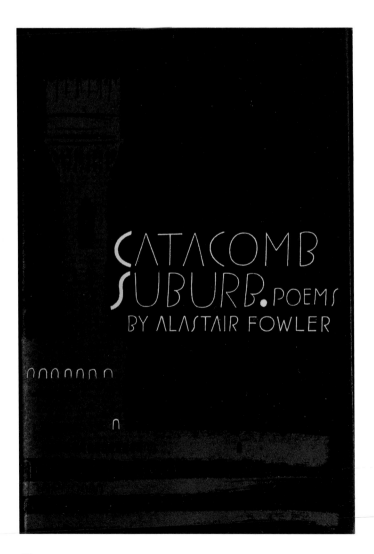

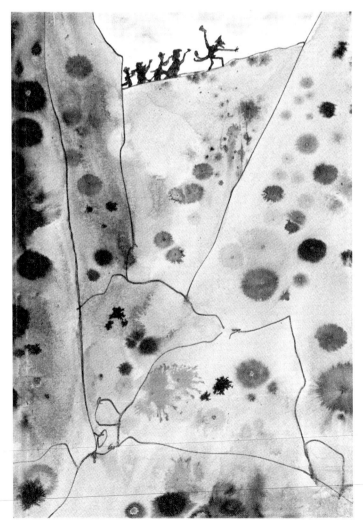

Quentin Blake
Binding design and illustration from *The Hunting of the Snark* by
Lewis Carroll, published by the Folio Society, 1976.

But while he was seeking with thimbles and care,
 A Bandersnatch swiftly drew nigh
And grabbed at the Banker, who shrieked in despair,
 For he knew it was useless to fly.

He offered large discount – he offered a cheque
 (Drawn 'to bearer') for seven-pounds-ten:
But the Bandersnatch merely extended its neck
 And grabbed at the Banker again.

Without rest or pause – while those frumious jaws
 Went savagely snapping around –
He skipped and he hopped, and he floundered and flopped,
 Till fainting he fell to the ground.

Kenneth Grange
Power Car Exterior for British Rail 125 High Speed Train, in service from 1976. The train was designed with the aim of promoting long distance high speed rail travel in competition with air and road transport. The 125 train consists of eight passenger cars with a driver's cab and power car at each end. During design development it was realised that it would be possible to dispense with the traditional buffers, since no shunting was required at turn round point. This contributed significantly to the distinctively styled and aerodynamically efficient design which emerged, based on wind-tunnel testing; and the shape of the 125 has been made much use of in establishing a more modern image for British Rail.

Tom Eckersley
London Transport Collection poster, 1975. Eckersley's first posters for London Transport – "By Bus to the Pictures Tonight" and so on – date back to c.1935. Fifty years later, his designs still have a comparable visual impact and sense of personality, bearing out his own dictum in his book *Poster Design* that the good poster is almost above fashion: *"Really fine work never dates: it is only posters which depend solely on the particular technique of their period which today appear dull and dated."*

London Transport Collection
The London Transport collection of historic vehicles: buses, trams, trolleybuses, locomotives, rolling stock, posters, signs, tickets and other exhibits at Syon Park, Brentford. Open every day except Christmas Day and Boxing Day. April to September 1000 – 1900, October to March 1000 – 1700 or dusk (whichever is earlier), admission 25p children 15p (last tickets issued one hour before closing). Underground to Hammersmith then bus 267, or to Gunnersbury then bus 117 or 267. On Sundays buses E1 and E2 run beyond Brentford to Syon Park. Green Line coach 701, British Rail to Gunnersbury or Kew Bridge, then buses 117 or 267; or to Syon Lane then short walk.

Alan Irvine
The Horses of San Marco, design for Olivetti exhibition at the Royal Academy, 1979.

Ted Happold
Umbrella structure designed for the U.S. Pink Floyd concert tour, 1980.

Tony Abbott
Set design for BBC TV production of *Timon of Athens* directed by Jonathan Miller, 1980.

Ralph Koltai
Set design for Royal Shakespeare Company production of *Much Ado About Nothing*, 1982.

Paul Hogarth
Book jackets for *Hamlet* and *Anthony and Cleopatra* in the Penguin New Shakespeare series, 1980. The links between RDIs and Penguin Books have always been particularly close, since the earliest Penguins with their Gill Sans type. Hans Schmoller, later an RDI, took over as typographical director in 1949 from Jan Tschichold, later an Hon. RDI; and many Penguin jackets have since then been illustrated or designed by a distinguished line of Royal Designers, among them Dennis Bailey and Derek Birdsall.

Michael Foreman
The Merchant of Venice, illustration from *Shakespeare Stories* published by Gollancz, 1985.

THE NEW PENGUIN

HAMLET

THE NEW PENGUIN

ANTONY AND CLEOPATRA

Martin Hunt
"Concept" teaset in vitrified earthenware designed for Hornsea Potteries in 1977. Martin Hunt of the Queensberry Hunt partnership set out to challenge the generally more sophisticated design standards of continental tableware, particularly German. "Concept" received a Design Council Award.
Design Council

Geoffrey Harcourt
"Michigan" high-back office chair from a series designed for Artifort 1983. Harcourt has designed seating for Artifort in Holland since 1962.
Artifort Press Service

Nicholas Butler
Durabeam torch range, designed between 1980 and 1984 for
Duracell Batteries Ltd. The Duracell torches, the result of bringing
designer's logic to bear on the multifarious products of the torch
industry, became cult objects of the 1980s as well as a considerable
marketing success.

David Carter
Range of screwdrivers designed for Stanley Tools Ltd., 1965.
The association of David Carter of DCA Consultants with Stanley
Tools through the 1960s and 1970s was exceptionally productive,
resulting in a collection of hand tools of the highest international
design standards.

David Mellor
''Atlanta'' cutlery in highly polished stainless steel, 1986.
This cutlery, designed and developed in Sheffield by David Mellor,
takes the traditional forms for eating implements and refines them
down to the minimum. This is the first time the classic English knife
has been made in a form suitable for use in high temperature
dishwashers.
Pete Hill

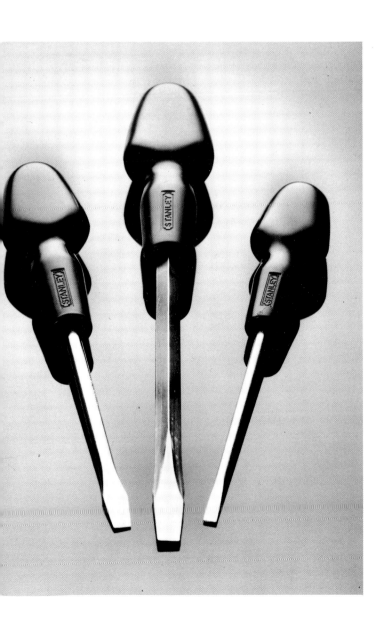

Zandra Rhodes
Dress from the "Ode to Woman" collection,
Autumn/Winter 1986. A silk chiffon dress
with hand-rolled edges and beaded points
and a low waistband in stitched satin.
The textile fabric is screen-printed by
hand, and the design shows the characteristic
Zandra Rhodes combination of
flamboyance and finesse.
Photograph: Robyn Beeche

Jean Muir
Dress from Autumn 1986 collection.
A matte jersey dress in navy blue which
typifies Jean Muir's architectural and
sculptural approach to making clothes.
Once an initial sketch has been made the
garment is constructed on the sewing
machine, a practical process similar to
that with which an engineer might tackle
a design project.
Sketch by Jean Muir

Extracts from the Ordinance of the Council of The Royal Society for the Encouragement of Arts, Manufactures and Commerce for the Conferment of Distinctions on Designers for Industry.

The Council may in their discretion and on behalf of the Society confer upon persons, being citizens of the United Kingdom, who have attained, in creative design for industry, eminence, efficiency and visual excellence, the following title, namely: Designer for Industry of the Royal Society of Arts (Royal Designer for Industry).

Every person upon whom such distinction may be conferred shall receive a diploma issued under authority of the Council on behalf of the Society, and may use the letters RDI *after his or her name as an indication thereof.*

Subject to such limitation in number as the Council may fix from time to time, the Council may confer on Designers, not being citizens of the United Kingdom, who have rendered signal service to industrial design the Honorary title of Designer for Industry of the Royal Society of Arts, *and such persons may use the letters* Hon RDI *after their respective names as an indication thereof.*

The number of persons bearing the distinction of Royal Designer for Industry on the Register at any time shall not be more than one hundred.

Honorary Royal Designers for Industry

From the very early years Honorary RDIs have been elected to the Faculty, a practice which has over the years drawn in many of the most famous practitioners of international modern design, and which throws interesting light on which designers have been most highly regarded by their British contemporaries.

Honorary RDIs:

1936	E. McKnight Kauffer, USA
1939	Edward Hald, Sweden
	Christian Joachim, Denmark
	Raymond Loewy, USA
1947	Alvar Aalto, Finland
	Walter Gropius, USA
	Steen Eiler Rasmussen, Denmark
1949	Kaare Klint, Denmark
	Astrid Sampe, Sweden
1951	Walter Dorwin Teague, USA
1954	Battista Pininfarina, Italy
1959	Hans J. Wegner, Denmark
1960	Charles Eames, USA
1961	Marcello Nizzoli, Italy
1963	Timo Sarpaneva, Finland
1964	Saul Bass, USA
	Tapio Wirkkala, Finland
1965	Alexander Hayden Girard, USA
	Jan Tschichold, Switzerland
1966	Piet Zwart, Holland
1968	Dieter Rams, West Germany
1969	Carlo Scarpa, Italy
	Ilmari Tapiovaara, Finland
1971	Franco Albini, Italy
	W. J. H. B. Sandberg, Holland
1972	Borge Mogensen, Denmark
1973	George Nelson, USA
	Paul Rand, USA
	Roger Tallon, France
1974	André François, France
1975	Olin Stephens, USA
	Henryk Tomaszewski, Poland
1976	Walter Herdeg, Switzerland
1978	Finn Juhl, Denmark
	Bruno Mathsson, Sweden
1979	Milton Glaser, USA
	Dora Jung, Finland
	Friso Kramer, Holland
1980	Richard Buckminster Fuller, USA
	Saul Steinberg, USA
1981	Jean Michel Folon, France
1982	Herbert Matter, Switzerland
1983	Takashi Kono, Japan
	Jack Lenor Larsen, USA
	Sergio Pininfarina, Italy
1984	C. L. "Kelly" Johnson, USA
	Herbert Bayer, USA
1985	Hermann Zapf, Germany
1986	Achille Castiglioni, Italy
	Shigeo Fukuda, Japan
	Norman McLaren, Canada
	Antti Nurmesniemi, Finland
	Maurice Sendak, USA

1936

Douglas Cockerell MBE (1870–1945).
Bookbinder. Born London. After a short career as farm-hand, wool-carder and banker in Canada, returned to England and became T. J. Cobden-Sanderson's first apprentice binder in 1893. Elected to Art Workers' Guild 1896. Taught at Central School until 1935, thereafter at RCA. Founded his own bindery in 1898, was controller of W. H. Smith's bindery 1904–14. Bound many rare manuscripts, chiefly for university libraries. Major work was probably the binding of the *Codex Sinaiticus* for the British Museum. Never concerned with the merely decorative, he has probably had more influence on bookbinding practice and design than any other one man.

Eric Gill ARA (1882–1940). *Sculptor, lettercutter, typographer and wood engraver.* Studied at Chichester Art School; abandoned architecture to develop his interest in lettering at the Central School under Johnston. Moved to Ditchling, Sussex, 1907; helped to create there a semi-monastic community of craftsmen. Moved to Capel-y-ffin, 1924, and to Pigotts, Buckinghamshire, 1928. Developed a deeply held if somewhat confused philosophy which greatly influenced his work, and his followers. His books gave him a great reputation as a penetrating thinker. His prolific and versatile output included several influential type designs. He was well aware of the conflict between his hatred of commerce and industry, and much of his work. There is sweet irony in Gill Sans becoming one of the types most widely used by commerce in the mid-twentieth century. Such conflicts still bother craftsmen and designers; and will presumably continue unless, as Gill demanded, society is restructured.

James Hogan (1883–1948). *Glass and stained glass designer.* Studied at the Central School and Camberwell. Member of Art Workers' Guild. As art director of James Powell & Sons (makers of Whitefriars glass) he designed glass for quantity production, hand-made glass, and stained-glass windows. Many of the latter were for American churches, but his most important commission was for the two 100-foot high windows for Gilbert Scott's Liverpool Cathedral.

J. H. Mason (1875–1951). *Printer and typographer.* Proof-reading boy at Ballantynes (London publisher) 1888. Apprenticed as compositor, stayed on as journeyman and became the company's expert in Greek and Latin. Joined Doves Press 1900, and worked on the Dover Bible. Taught printing and typography at the Central School from 1905. Founded *The Imprint* (with F. E. Jackson, Johnston and G. Meynell). Designed "Imprint" for Monotype Corporation 1913 – which began its influential type design programme. Assisted in the setting up of The Cranach Press, Weimar, 1913.

H. G. Murphy (1884–1939). *Goldsmith and silversmith.* Studied at Central School. Assistant to Henry Wilson, sculptor, metalworker and jeweller, 1900. Taught at the Central, to become head of Silversmithing Department, and finally Principal of the school. He continued with his own productive craft workshop, giving a subtle contemporary flavour to traditional forms.

Keith Murray MC (1892–1981). *Glass, pottery and silverware designer.* Born New Zealand, came to England 1906–7. Trained as architect at the AA. Gained a three-months-a-year contract with Stevens & Williams Glassworks 1932, and a similar contract with Wedgwood 1933. Designed a great number of immensely successful shapes and decorations for both companies. Worked for Mappin & Webb from 1934. Recommenced architecture 1936, still occasionally designing for Wedgwood. His simple, refined, matt-glazed pottery for Wedgwood has become almost a symbol of 1930s modernism.

Tom Purvis (1888–1959). *Graphic designer.* Born Bristol, studied painting at Camberwell. Designer in a London advertising agency for six years before freelancing. A prolific poster designer in the days when the job was called "commercial art". Did much influential work for LNER, London Underground, Shell, and Austin Reed, steering poster design away from realism to a more symbolic treatment, with broad massing of strong colours and the elimination of detail. Official war artist in World War II, producing posters of war work in factories, urging general uplift.

George Sheringham (**1884–1937**). *Interior and textile designer.* Studied art at the Slade, and in Paris. Originally a painter, by 1911 was designing fans and silk panels. Best known as a theatre designer, particularly for his work at the Lyric Theatre, Hammersmith. Also a successful architectural decorator (Claridges Ballroom 1931), textile designer, and carpet designer for John Crossley. He continued his painting career alongside these and other activities (posters, advertising, book illustration), allowing it to influence them.

Harold Stabler (**1872–1945**). *Potter, enameller, silversmith.* Born at Levens, Westmorland, apprenticed to a Kendal woodcarver for seven years, then studied metalwork at Keswick School of Art. Came to London in early 1900s, taught at RCA 1912–26; head of Art Department, Sir John Cass Institute, 1907–37. In 1921 became a partner of Carter & Co. Pottery, Poole. Worked on war memorials, decorative figures, tiles, tableware, including Pyrex glassware; designed and executed silverware. Despite such craftwork, was a dogged spokesman for improvement in the designs of everyday, machine-made, things – an attitude which did not endear him to some of his fellow craftsmen.

Fred Taylor (**1875–1963**). *Graphic designer.* Born London, studied at Goldsmith's College. Watercolour artist. Designed a long series of fine posters for LNER, London Underground, and other railways (frequently of architectural subjects). They were often scenes of considerable elaboration, firmly organised, executed in a strong, simplified style. Involved in camouflage work in World War I.

C. F. A. Voysey (**1857–1941**). *Architect; interior, furniture and fabric designer.* Pupil of J. P. Seddon, assistant to George Devey, he set up his own architectural office in 1884, pursuing an individual interpretation of Arts & Crafts themes. His strong original forms were infused with an inspired interpretation of traditional vernacular details – making him very much an architect for today. He began to design furniture, wallpaper and textiles in 1888, often based on simplified natural patterns. A perfec-

tionist, he believed that fittings and furniture should be considered with the architecture. Some of his designs were for mass production, and were among the most commercially successful of their period. Unwilling to compromise his continuing Arts & Crafts beliefs, he did very little design or architectural work in the changed atmosphere after World War I.

1937

Reco Capey (**1895–1961**). *Industrial and packaging designer.* Born in Burslem, studied at the RCA, in France, in Italy and in Sweden. Designer of pottery, glass, metal, textiles, lacquer etc; but best known as art director for Yardley, 1928–38. Chief Instructor in Design at RCA 1924–35.

E. Gordon Craig CH (**1872–1966**). *Stage designer.* Born Stevenage. His mother was Ellen Terry. Initially an actor. In 1900 he designed and directed Purcell's *Dido and Aeneas*, a startlingly original production. Both this and his next productions, exploiting his visionary ideas on the use of light and colour, and his belief in a unified theatrical experience under the control of one mastermind, were commercial failures; although great successes among artists. A somewhat tempestuous personal life was mostly lived abroad. His *Hamlet* at the Arts Theatre, Moscow 1911, was a triumph; but after an elaborate final venture – Ibsen's *The Pretenders*, Copenhagen 1926 – he concentrated on his books, his brilliant woodcuts, and his talk: a stage "the thwarted genius" could really exploit.

Milner Gray CBE (**1899–**). *Graphic and industrial designer.* Born Blackheath. Studied painting and design at Goldsmith's College. Founder member of SIA, 1930; senior partner Bassett-Gray/Industrial Design Partnership 1922–40; founder partner of DRU from 1943, senior consultant since 1980. During World War II he worked together with Misha Black and others of his old associates for the Ministry of Information, designing propaganda exhibitions. Has been a leading member, chairman, or president, of almost every national and international body in graphic design and industrial design. From the 1940s onwards, pursuing a policy to present "a service so complete it could undertake any design case which might confront the State, Municipal Authorities, Industry or Commerce", he has been responsible for innumerable wide-ranging and influential schemes.

Ethel Mairet (1872–1952). *Weaver.* Born Barnstaple, Devon. Little formal training for textile work. Lived Ceylon 1903–6 (an experience to have great influence on her future work); and Chipping Campden 1906–10. In close contact with C. R. Ashbee and the Guild of Handicraft. Started weaving 1911–12, in Devon. Moved to Ditchling, Sussex (where Eric Gill was also working) in 1918. Her workshop became a creative centre for weavers from many countries. Particularly knowledgeable about vegetable dyes, she was also concerned about the relationship of hand weaving to power loom production.

Percy Metcalfe CVO (1895–1970). *Designer of coins and medals.* Studied at the RCA. Won the competition for a keepsake medal for the British Empire Exhibition, Wembley 1924. His animal designs for Irish coinage 1928 were welcomed by many as exemplary modern coinage; but he seemed less successful in England.

1939

Sir Ambrose Heal (1872–1959). *Furniture designer.* Born London. After studying at the Slade, served an apprenticeship as a cabinet maker, then joined the family firm in 1893. A fine craftsman, he began to design furniture in the Arts & Crafts manner, with a fondness for solid oak and simplicity. Member of the Art Workers' Guild. From 1930s, he adopted a more modern approach to furniture, following his designers J. E. Johnson and Arthur Greenwood. Always a figurehead of good design, particularly throughout the 1920s and 1930s, he was also an astute businessman. Resigned chairmanship of Heal's in 1953, although he remained a director until his death.

Laurence Irving OBE (1897–). *Stage and film designer.* After World War 1 he studied as a painter at the Royal Academy Schools. He designed his first settings and costumes for the stage in 1925. In 1928 Douglas Fairbanks Snr invited him to Hollywood to design the settings for his last silent film *The Man In The Iron Mask*. Returning to Hollywood in 1929 he designed, in collaboration with William Cameron Menzies, the settings and costumes for the first sound film production – *Taming of the Shrew* – for Fairbanks and Mary Pickford. Thereafter in England he pioneered the role of Production Designer and the technique for script illustration (storyboard illustration) which he introduced to the British film industry, notably for Pascal's films of Shaw's *Pygmalion, The Doctor's Dilemma* (project) and *Major Barbara.* After the war he continued designing for film and stage productions until 1953.

Brian O'Rorke RA (1901–1974). *Architect and interior designer.* Born New Zealand, studied architecture at Cambridge University and the AA. Uncompromisingly modern, he ran a small independent practice, specialising in interior design, particularly for ships, aircraft and trains. In the 1930s he designed interiors of ss *Orion* and ss *Orcades*, which broke away from previous deeply traditional approaches. He subsequently designed further Orient Line ships, the interior of the Vickers Viking in 1946, and was architect for the Orient Line Building in Sydney, 1947.

1940

Susie Cooper OBE (1902–). *Ceramic designer.* Born 1902 in Staffordshire. After training at the Burslem School of Art under Gordon Forsythe she joined A. E. Gray as a decorator of ceramics. Having risen to be the company's chief designer, she left in 1929 to found her own pottery in Burslem. Having rapidly established her own style of elegant but utilitarian shapes and decoration, she was one of the major innovators in domestic ceramics through the 1930s. Appointed RDI in 1940. A fire in her factory during the war meant an enforced three-year lay off, but she returned to greater eminence and continued innovation in ceramic design through the 1940s and 1950s. She created, for example, the tableware for the Royal Pavilion at the Festival of Britain and her products enjoyed great acclaim in both domestic and export markets. In 1966 her company was taken over by Josiah Wedgwood and Sons for whom she has

E. Gordon Craig

Susie Cooper

remained a senior and much loved designer for the past 20 years. She was awarded the OBE in 1979.

E. W. Grieve. *Shop window display designer.* Display manager for Harrods in the period immediately before World War II.

A. B. Read (**1899–1973**). *Industrial and light-fitting designer.* Studied metalwork at the RCA 1919–23. His interest in Gropius's work led him to visit the Bauhaus. After working with the French lighting firm of Bagnés 1924–25, he became consultant designer and director of Troughton & Young, where he gained a reputation as a pioneer in the design of light fittings. He was later also retained as a designer by the Carter Group of Poole. Working with many architects of the Modern Movement in the 1920s and 1930s, he did much to alter the character of interior lighting.

Sir Gordon Russell CBE MC (**1892–1980**). *Furniture maker and designer.* Born Cricklewood. Family moved to Broadway, Worcestershire, 1904. In charge of a small antiques-restoration workshop 1908; began practising a number of crafts. Designed furniture in the manner of Ernest Gimson. Set up Gordon Russell Ltd 1926, and began to mechanise, attempting to reconcile the best of the Arts & Crafts tradition with efficient machine production. Very influential on official design policy from 1939 onwards (Utility furniture, Council of Industrial Design, Festival of Britain). His firm's furniture, of fine quality, was never (apart from his brother's designs for Murphy radio in the 1930s) intended for the popular market, though he himself was much concerned to raise standards for "the great mass of the people".

Percy Delf Smith (**1882–1948**). *Letterer.* Born London, studied painting at Camberwell, then book illustration, and lettering under Johnston and Grailey Hewitt. Set up workshop 1914, working alongside his craftsmen. After World War I, his Dorian Studio specialised in war memorials, including the sandblasting through stencils of 11,700 names for the Canadian Memorial at Vimy Ridge. Continued to produce high-quality inscriptions, and innumerable small-scale printed items. Also a book designer of the romantic, decorative school, designing vignettes, bindings, printers' flowers. Etcher and engraver. Member of the Art Workers' Guild.

Allan Walton (**1891–1948**). *Textile designer and manufacturer.* Trained with a London architect, then studied painting at the Slade and Westminster (under Sickert) and in Paris. Painter, designer, decorator and architect, decorated Boulestin 1925, then, with his brother, set up Allan Walton Textiles. As Director, commissioned some of the most enterprising artist-designed screen-printed fabrics of the 1930s (Vanessa Bell, Duncan Grant). Also designed embroideries, carpets and fabrics himself. Influential propagandist for good design. Director of Glasgow School of Art 1943–45.

Anna Zinkeisen (**1906–1976**). *Graphic designer and mural painter.* Born Kilcreggan, Dunbartonshire. In 1921 studied painting, and later sculpture, at RA Schools. In 1924 (still only 18) set up studio with her sister Doris, beginning a versatile professional life, covering portraiture, magazine and book covers, illustration, commercial design and mural painting. Meticulously recorded the London Blitz in World War II, and did pathological and clinical drawings for surgeons. Executed large murals for hospitals, and for the liners *Queen Mary* and *Queen Elizabeth* at their refit.

1941
Duncan Grant (**1885–1978**). *Painter and designer.* Born Rothiemurchus, Inverness. Painting at Westminster and Slade; 1907–9 lived in Paris. 1913–19 co-director of Omega Workshops (set up by Roger Fry to enable young artists to make a living) designing textiles, pottery etc, and painting furniture. Inventive and versatile; a central figure of "Bloomsbury". In the 1920s and 1930s collaborated with Vanessa Bell in interior schemes, designing rugs, printed furnishings, embroideries, tableware, generally in a painterly, rather "splodgy" style. Had a remarkable talent for inventing ornamentation upon almost any surface. Three panels for the *Queen Mary* were rejected by Cunard Chairman for being too "modern".

1943

Charles Holden (1875–1960). *Architect and transport equipment designer.* Born Bolton. Apprenticed to architect E. W. Leeson, and studied at Manchester. Briefly with C. R. Ashbee from 1897, then Percy Adams, entering into partnership after their design for Bristol Library 1906. One of four principal architects for War Graves Commission. Stylistically uncommitted. In 1924 began 15 years of happy collaboration with Frank Pick at London Transport, having travelled in Germany, Holland, Denmark, Sweden to evaluate developments there. On his return, he used a distinctive, unaggressively contemporary manner. Frequently commissioned work from sculptors such as Epstein, Gill, Moore. From 1931 he designed new buildings for London University: perhaps not so esteemed today as when they were built. After World War II, concentrated on town planning.

Sir Barnes Wallis CBE FRS (1887–1979). *Engineer and aircraft designer.* Trained as marine engineer; joined airship department of Vickers in 1913. Chief airship designer 1916. Designed highly successful R100 in 1925, pioneering early form of geodetic construction later developed for Vickers Wellesley and Wellington. During World War II he invented several bombs, including the dam-breaching bouncing bomb. Made valuable contributions to development of supersonic aircraft. Invented *Swallow* variable-sweep wing principle (like many of his visionary ideas, passed over by his own country).

1944

Wells Coates OBE (1895–1958). *Architect and industrial designer.* Born of Canadian parents in Tokyo, educated in Japan; studied engineering at McGill University Canada 1913. After World War I, worked in Canada as journalist and lumberjack; worked with architects in London and Paris, 1923–26. Began working on his own in London about 1927, first on interiors, later also as architect and industrial designer. Designed some elegant modern shops. Consultant architect to Jack Pritchard's Isokon Co. from 1930; founded MARS Group 1933. Initiated England into the International Style with his Lawn Road Flats, Hampstead. Designed radio sets for Ecko 1932 onwards – the first authentically modern appliance design in Britain. Also furniture, and studio interiors for Broadcasting House. Innovative and influential architect/designer of the 1930s; produced little after World War II, practising largely in Canada.

Sir Geoffrey de Havilland OM CBE (1882–1965). *Aircraft designer.* Trained as motor engineer until 1908, but switched to aircraft, designing and building a biplane which he sold to the government. Joined Army Balloon Factory, designed the first of the BE (British Experimental) series. In 1914 became Chief Designer and Test Pilot, Aircraft Manufacturing Co., producing the DH series of fighters. Five went into large-scale production during World War I. Set up de Havilland Aircraft Co. in 1920, resulting in a long series of both aero engines and of highly successful and unusually elegant aircraft: the various Moths, Dragon Rapide, Comet racer, Albatross (killed by World War II), Mosquito (using the wood construction of the Albatross, but here a bold solution to production problems and metal shortage), and the pioneering but doomed Comet.

Enid Marx (1902–). *Textile and graphic designer, printmaker, illustrator.* Born London, daughter of Robert J. Marx, innovative engineer. Roedean, Central School (drawing, pottery, printed textiles), RCA (painting, wood engraving). After working with Barron and Larcher 1925–27, had her own textile printing workshop until 1939. A versatile designer, particularly of decorative items: pattern papers (for books and wrapping), book jackets (Chatto & Windus, Penguin), illustrations, trademarks, printed and woven fabrics, wallpapers, posters (London Transport), calendars (Shell), ceramics, plastics, logos, postage stamps. 1944–47 member of Utility Furniture Advisory Panel, designing a series of furnishing fabrics. Enthusiast for and propagandist of English popular and traditional arts.

Charles Nicholson OBE (1868–1954). *Yacht designer.* Born Gosport. Launched his first design at 18, first success a few years later.

1962, designed *Istria*, reintroducing the Bermuda rig. Designed *Shamrock IV* for Sir Thomas Lipton's challenge for the America's Cup, but World War I intervened and she was defeated in 1920. Designed *Endeavour* for Sopwith's challenge – "the most beautiful racing yacht ever built" – but she too was (narrowly) defeated in 1934. Versatile and prolific, the foremost designer of racing yachts. Played a pioneer part in the development of the motor yacht; his success diverted the demand for Clyde-built steam yachts to Gosport- or Southampton-built motor yachts. *Philante* of 1937 was largest UK-built motor yacht; now Norwegian Royal Yacht.

Professor R. D. Russell (1903–1981).

Architect and furniture designer. Brother of Gordon Russell. AA, then joined Gordon Russell Ltd 1929, designing dining-room and bedroom furniture, sideboards, chests and, notably, radio cabinets. Staff industrial designer with Murphy Radio 1934–36; consultant from 1936. Continued in private practice after Word War II, and also was influential teacher at RCA. Remodelled Greek Sculpture Galleries at British Museum, 1960s; Western Sculpture, Print Room, and Oriental Art Galleries (all with R. Y. Goodden) 1969–71.

1945
Sir Francis Meynell (1891–1975).

Typographer. Born London. Trinity College Dublin 1909–11. Designer at Burns & Oates, Catholic publishers, 1911–13. Stanley Morison was his assistant. Edited *The Communist* newspaper 1918–20; also assistant editor and director of *The Herald*. Founded Nonesuch Press 1923, revived it 1951–72 (the Press being taken over by Limited Editions Club, 1935–51). Commissioned designs from George Grosz, McKnight Kauffer, Rudolf Koch, Paul Nash, Reynolds, Stone, etc. Nonesuch bridged the gap between private presses and commercial book production, using modern methods to obtain high quality at moderate prices. Also did freelance advertising design. After World War II, was typographic adviser to HMSO, and Director-General of the Cement & Concrete Association.

1947
James Gardner CBE (1907–). *Exhibition and general designer.* Born London. Jewellery designer for Cartier 1924–31. Chief Deception Officer during World War II. Versatile and prolific independent designer since 1947, responsible for numerous trade and educational exhibitions (Britain Can Make It 1946; Pleasure Gardens, Battersea 1951; UK Pavilion, Brussels World Fair 1958; Commonwealth Institute 1962; and fifteen museums throughout the world). Output includes an exploding bicycle pump, and the visual design of *Queen Elizabeth II*.

Professor R. Y. Goodden CBE (1909–).

Architect and general designer. AA 1926–31, in private practice from 1932. Varied output includes: wallpapers; domestic pressed glassware for Chance Bros; the Sports Section of Britain Can Make It 1946; Lion & Unicorn Building, Festival of Britain 1951 (with R. D. Russell); coronation hangings, Westminster Abbey 1953; gold and silver ware; ceremonial metal work; glassware for Kings College Cambridge; metal foil murals for ss *Canberra* 1961; engraved and sand-blasted glass murals for Pilkington's; Western Sculpture, Print Room and Oriental Galleries at the British Museum (all with R. D. Russell) 1969–71. Was Professor of Silversmithing, RCA 1948–74.

Ashley Havinden OBE (1903–1973).

Graphic and textile designer. Evening classes at Central School. Joined Crawford's advertising agency 1922 as trainee; Director of Art and Design 1929; Vice Chairman 1960–67. 1933 began to design rugs and textiles. His campaign for Chrysler, initiated 1925, utilised bold sanserifs and imagery reflecting cubist and futurist painting. Particularly influential in the 1930s: Milk Marketing Board, GPO, Simpson's. Post-war work included Richard Shops, DAKS, Wolsey, Pretty Polly. Freelanced 1967–73. Ashley's distinctive style was free, casual-seeming and elegant. His undogmatic approach was receptive to the influence of fine art; but such influence was always well-digested.

1948

Christian Barman OBE (1898–1980).
Architect, product designer, transport equipment. Of Swedish family, studied architecture at Liverpool University. Edited *AJ* and *AR*. Product designer in 1930s. Appointed publicity officer to LPTB 1935–41. Partnering Frank Pick, was responsible for visual presentation. He himself designed many items (bus shelters, canopies, etc). Commissioned designs for street and station furniture, signs, printed matter and train interiors. 1947–62, Chief Publicity Officer to British Transport Commission, setting up Railway Design Panel in 1953. A pioneer of design management, he promoted good design by quiet but relentless persuasion.

1949

Edward Bawden CBE RA (1903–). *Painter, printmaker, graphic designer, illustrator.* Studied at Cambridge from 1919, RCA 1922–25. Mural decorations (with Eric Ravilious) for Morley College 1928–29. Prolific illustrator, notably for Shell, Fortnum & Mason, Imperial Airways, Orient Line, Twinings Tea; work now redolent of the 1930s. His wallpaper designs for Cole & Son were printed from lino-cut blocks; posters for London Transport also exploited the medium: he raised this elementary school technique to the status of fine art. Has illustrated countless books. Versatile artist who recognises no boundaries between fine art and commercial work – and moves easily between various commercial disciplines. War artist, World War II. An impressive craftsman, with a firm line, strong sense of pattern, and (particularly) a daft, gently malicious humour. A modern Edward Lear in his work; but thinner.

Barnett Freedman CBE (1901–1958).
Painter, lithographer, graphic designer. Son of Russian Jews living in Stepney. Evening classes at St. Martin's 1917–22, RCA 1922–25. Revived colour lithography (illustrations to *Memoirs of an Infantry Officer* 1931). Many book jackets, and posters, etc. for London Transport, Shell, GPO (notably George V Jubilee Stamp 1935). His work covered a wide range of printed ephemera, including cotton reel labels. War artist

World War II. Sheer ability and persistence overcame poverty and ill health. A gifted illustrator, his other work often incorporated his own distinctive (and excellent) lettering, worlds away from Arts & Crafts preciousness.

Roger Furse (1903–1972). *Stage and film designer.* Studied painting at Slade, then Paris, then lived and worked in US for five years. Returned to UK 1932; began designing sets and costumes for the London theatre. Gained a reputation for period recreation. From 1938 was closely associated with the Old Vic. In 1944 was released from Navy to design Olivier's film of *Henry V*. Also designed *Odd Man Out, Hamlet, Richard III* etc., while continuing his stage work (especially with Olivier). Designed for opera and ballet too. His work was discreet, varied, and sensitive to each production's requirements.

Eric C. Ottaway (1904–1967). *Road transport designer.* Trained as mechanical engineer, joined Midland Red Bus in 1925. In 1929, assistant experimental engineer, London General Omnibus (to become LPTB). During World War II in aircraft production management. Returning to London Transport, was largely responsible for the design of post-war buses and coaches. Also on LT's Design Panel, concerned with vehicle design, especially new Underground stock for Victoria Line.

1950

Sir James McNeill KCVO CBE MC FRS (1892–1964). *Ship designer.* Apprentice draughtsman at John Brown's shipyard, Clydebank, 1908. He later graduated at Glasgow University in naval architecture and engineering. After World War I, returned to John Brown as assistant naval architect; 1928, chief naval architect. 1953, Managing Director. Co-ordinator of design for *Queen Mary* and *Queen Elizabeth*; co-designer of Royal Yacht *Britannia*.

Edward Molyneux MC (1891–1974). *Dress designer.* Born London of Irish parents. Worked for London fashion house of Lucille. After World War I, opened his own fashion house in Paris. His classy clothes, well made and understated, were a great

success. Expanded to Monte Carlo, 1925, and London, 1933. The London branch exported $2 million worth of fashion to USA between June 1940 and April 1941. His influence percolated down through the whole fashion industry.

1951
Sir Hugh Casson CH KCVO RA (1910–).
Architect and exhibition designer. Born London. Cambridge 1929–31; architecture at UCL 1931–32, and at British School, Athens, 1933. In private practice from 1933; senior partner, Casson Conder Partnership from 1946. Director of Architecture, Festival of Britain 1951. The firm's many notable buildings include the Elephant House at London Zoo; RCA building; Islamic Centre, South Kensington; has been particularly associated with universities, and projects of historic conservation. Interiors include various Royal Apartments, and areas in ss *Canberra*. Also designed many stage productions (ROH Covent Garden, Glyndebourne). Solutions often derive their visual treatment from their especial associations, and are unusually sensitive to their surroundings. Taught at RCA 1953–75. President of RA 1976–84.

J. Laurent Giles (1901–1969). *Yacht designer.*
Studied engineering at Cambridge; joined Vickers Armstrong at Newcastle, then Camper and Nicholson. In 1927 founded Laurent Giles & Partners, with varied and prolific output. Developed cruising yachts (Vertue class etc.), then ocean racers such as *Maid of Malham*. After work on small naval craft in World War II, he developed light ocean racers such as *Myth of Malham*, which twice won the Fastnet, while continuing work in all areas of yacht design.

1953
Ernest Race (1913–1964). *Furniture designer.*
Born Newcastle. Studied interior design at Bartlett School London 1932–35. Model maker 1935, then lighting designer under A. B. Read, Troughton & Young, 1936–37. Founded Race Fabrics 1937, selling textiles of his design, hand-woven in India. Co-founder of Race Furniture 1945. Had an innovative attitude to materials, and produced a succession of famous chairs,

especially of metal, making expressive use of steel rods. Several designs were used in Festival of Britain 1951, where they popularised the contemporary spikey look. Also worked in plywood.

John Waterer (1892–1977). *Leather goods designer.*
Managing Director of S. Clark & Co. Designer and producer of luggage and leather goods. Instigator of the use of the zip fastener for luggage, and inventor of the modern lightweight suitcase.

1954
Sir William Lyons (1901–1985). *Car designer.*
Born Blackpool. Opened small factory 1922 building Swallow sidecars; expanded to include car coachwork. 1928 moved to Coventry. His first complete car, the SS (Swallow Sports) emerged 1931. 1935, first Jaguar saloon. Built first series production car capable of over 100 mph for under £450. 1945 company became Jaguar Cars Ltd, producing a series of high-quality sports cars and saloons, at the lowest possible price. Autocratic and dictatorial, but he had worked at the drawing-board in every phase of car design.

1955
Uffa Fox CBE (1898–1972). *Small-boat designer.*
Born Cowes, at 14 was apprenticed to boatbuilder S. E. Saunders. During World War I worked on flying boats and seaplanes. About 1920, set up his own firm, designing dozens of boats, including the Firefly and Albacore classes, and the East Anglian sliding-seat canoe. He broke completely with tradition in his dinghy design: the planing dinghy (Flying Fifteen) transformed sailing from a rich man's pastime to a popular sport; his influential Avenger had a V-shaped hull. In World War II he designed the parachuted airborne lifeboat of plywood, which automatically unfolded on descent, was self-righting, self-bailing, protected up to 25 men from exposure, had engine and fuel for 1,000 miles, food and clothing for a month.

1956
Reynolds Stone CBE (1909–1979). *Letterer and wood engraver.*
Born Eton, studied history at Cambridge. Apprentice compositor at CUP 1930–32; compositor for a small

jobbing printer 1932–34. Freelance typographer, book designer, calligrapher and wood-engraver from 1934; letter cutter from 1939. Designed Royal Arms for HMSO, lettering for Nonesuch Press, stamps for GPO, banknotes, and numerous symbols and devices. Illustrated many books with particularly sensitive wood engravings, especially of the English countryside. With a somewhat limited repertoire of letterforms, usually engraved in wood or carved in stone, his swirls and flourishes became practically a trademark.

1957
Professor Sir Misha Black OBE (1910–1977).
Industrial and exhibition designer. Born Baku, Azerbaydzhan, Russia. Came to UK 1912. Mainly self taught. Architect and designer in London from 1929 (radio sets to Kardomah coffee shops). Partner with Milner Gray in Industrial Design Partnership 1933–39, the first multi-skill design group. Exhibition designer for Ministry of Information 1940–45. Co-founder, also with Milner Gray, of DRU 1945. Vast output, specialising in corporate design, and ranging from interiors, with their furnishing and equipment, to engineering products and locomotives. Fluent and highly articulate speaker, accomplished organiser and design propagandist. Influential Professor of Industrial Design, RCA 1959–75.

1959
Robin Day OBE (1915–). *Furniture and exhibition designer.*
Born High Wycombe. Local art school 1930–33, RCA 1934–38. Freelance since 1945. Design consultant for Hille since 1950, producing designs for much contract furniture culminating in his polypropylene chair of 1962, a modern classic, 12 million sold. Consultant for the John Lewis Partnership (from 1962). Other work includes design of section of Festival of Britain, seating for Royal Festival Hall 1951, Milan Triennale exhibitions 1951, 1953 (gold and silver medals), interiors of Super VC10 and other aircraft, seating for many auditoriums including Barbican Arts Centre. Concerned with designing low-cost well-designed products for quantity production.

Abram Games OBE (1914–). *Poster and graphic designer.* Born London. Self-taught designer, working in London studios 1932–36, then freelance, designing posters and publicity for Shell, London Transport, GPO, industry and government. Private in the Infantry 1940–41; drafted to War Office as first official poster designer, producing nearly 100 celebrated examples. Resumed freelancing 1946. Designed over 280 posters, numerous emblems and stamps. Influenced by cubist and surrealist painters, but never afraid of commercialism and the hard sell. For whatever market, the images are pared down to their most basic and forceful form, while often incorporating subtle symbolism. His personal philosophy: "maximum meaning, minimum means".

F. H. K. Henrion OBE (1914–). *Graphic designer and corporate identity consultant.* Born Nuremberg, studied graphic design at Ecole Paul Colin, Paris 1934–36; emigrated to UK, designing exhibitions before and during World War II (Ministry of Information, US Office of War Information). Consultant to advertising agencies and publishers from 1942 until late 1950s. Frequently incorporated surrealist concepts in his work at this time. Principal of Henrion Design Associates 1951–82, and consultant to Henrion Ludlow & Schmidt since 1982, covering almost all forms of graphic and industrial design. An international designer-communicator and a pioneer of corporate identity programmes. Forceful, simple ideas, executed in relaxed graphic means: his French design education is often apparent.

Hans Schleger (1898–1976). *Graphic designer.* Born Kempen, Germany. Studied painting and drawing in Berlin 1918–21. Publicity manager and film set designer Berlin 1921–24; magazine paste-up artist and freelance advertising designer New York 1924–29. Berlin advertising agency 1929–32. Settled in England 1932 as freelance, working for London Transport, Shell, GPO, Ministry of Agriculture, Ministry of Transport, ROSPA, Martini, American Overseas Airlines; corporate identities for MacFisheries, AEI, ICI, Fisons, Jaeger, Grants Whisky, Edinburgh International Festival, John Lewis, Finmar Furniture, etc. Used the work-name "Zero".

Dr Berthold Wolpe OBE (1905–). *Typographer and letterer.* Type and graphic designer, and lecturer. Studied under Rudolf Koch at Offenbach 1924–27. Was his assistant 1929–34. Taught at art schools: Offenbach 1929–33, Frankfurt 1930–33. Designed Hyperion type 1931. First visit to London 1932, when he met Stanley Morison who commissioned him to design a new printing type based on Wolpe's bronze inscriptions. Came to England for good in 1935. Worked at Fanfare Press for Ernest Ingham 1935–40. Designed Tempest type 1936 and Fanfare type ornaments 1938. Joined Faber & Faber 1941, designing books, bindings and jackets. Teaching at Camberwell 1948–53. Tutor at Royal College of Art 1956–65, visiting lecturer there 1965–75. Still teaching at City & Guilds of London Art School. His printing types also include Sachsenwald 1937, Decorata 1950, an italic type commissioned by LTB to match its Johnston Sans Serif Roman 1973 and the families of Albertus 1932–84 and Pegasus 1937–84. The last two groups of types have now been digitised.

1960

Stanley Morison (1889–1967). *Typographer.* Born Wanstead, Essex. Clerical work until 1906. Assistant editor *The Imprint* 1913–14. Assistant to Francis Meynell at Burns & Oates, Catholic publishers, 1918–19. Designer at Meynell's Pelican Press 1919–21; Cloister Press 1921–23. Typography adviser to Monotype Corporation 1923–67, where he had immense and beneficial influence on British printing, responsible for Monotype's unparalleled range of archetypal designs. Adviser to CUP 1924–30. Typography adviser to *The Times* 1929–60, effecting dramatic changes in its appearance. Also freelance book designer, principally for Gollancz, from 1923 (designing unexpectedly aggressive jackets). An active and erudite propagandist for good, if somewhat traditional, typography.

Alastair Morton (1910–1963). *Textile designer.* Joined the family firm Morton Sundour Fabrics 1931. Supervised the first Sundour screen-printed fabrics. Artistic director, presiding genius and principal designer of Edinburgh Weavers (a subsidiary

of Morton Sundour) from 1932. Despite the name, the weaving sheds were in Carlisle. In the forefront of the Modern Movement, 1930s-60s, commissioning designs from notable painters and designers. Also designed dress fabrics for Horrockses.

Sir Basil Spence OM OBE RA (1907–1976). *Architect, exhibition and interior designer.* Born Bombay of an Orkney family. Studied architecture at Edinburgh and London. Draughtsman for Lutyens during design of Viceroy's House, Delhi. Prior to World War II, built large country houses. Busy practice since World War II: housing estates, churches, theatres, schools, civic centres, Coventry Cathedral, Sussex University; Chief Architect, Britain Can Make It 1946; Scottish Industries Exhibition 1949; Sea & Ships Pavilion, Festival of Britain 1951; British Pavilion, Expo 67 at Montreal; many other exhibitions.

1961

Stefan Buzas (1915–). *Architect, exhibition and interior designer.* Born Hungary, studied architecture at Vienna. Came to England 1938, studied at AA. Taught at AA, Kingston, and North Carolina. Partner, James Cubitt & Partners, 1949–64; work includes displays in Dome of Discovery 1951, houses, shops and travel offices (four in Piccadilly alone in 1950s). Partner of Buzas & Irvine since 1965, specialising in smaller-scale work, especially interiors and exhibitions, of great perfection and economy of means.

Jack Howe (1911–). *Architect, engineering and industrial designer.* Studied at Polytechnic School of Architecture; assistant to Maxwell Fry and Walter Gropius 1933–39. Associate Partner, Arcon, 1944–48. Private practice 1949; partnership with Andrew Bain 1959–76. Designed schools, housing, exhibitions; industrial design consultant to various large firms (electric and electronic equipment, electron microscope x-ray equipment, turbines etc.), and British Rail (diesel electric locomotives, Pullman trains, railway equipment). A pioneering industrial designer in UK.

1962

Lucienne Day (1917–). *Textile designer.* Born Surrey. Croydon School of Art 1934–37, RCA 1937–40. Taught at Beckenham 1942–47. Freelance since 1948, designing dress and furnishing fabrics, carpets, wallpapers, table linens. Has designed for Edinburgh Weavers, Heal's (for 25 years), Wilton Royal Carpets, John Lewis, and other major firms at both home and abroad. Designed porcelain decorations for Rosenthal 1957–69. Has recently moved towards craftwork, producing one-off silk mosaic tapestries since 1978. Respects both craft traditions and quality bulk production requirements. Often collaborates with her husband Robin Day, including the consultancy for John Lewis.

David Mellor OBE (1930–). *Industrial designer.* Born Sheffield. Sheffield College of Art 1946–48, RCA 1950–54. Set up own silversmithing/industrial design workshop in Sheffield 1954. Developed design practice with emphasis on metalwork, from special silver for British embassies to bus shelters, traffic signals and machine tool design. Has always specialised in cutlery. First consultancy with Walker and Hall, Sheffield, for whom he designed Pride. Started manufacturing his own cutlery designs in early 1970s at Broom Hall, Sheffield, using innovative methods. Simultaneously opened David Mellor shops, selling kitchenware and tableware of modern functional design.

1963

Tom Eckersley OBE (1914–). *Graphic designer.* Born Newton-le-Willows, Lancashire. Salford School of Art 1930–34. Partnership with Eric Lombers, London 1934–40: work for London Transport, Shell, GPO, BBC, Austin Reed. Cartographer in RAF 1940–45, also designing many posters for ROSPA, GPO, Ministry of Information. Freelance since 1945, with poster design as main activity. Also head of Graphic Design Department, London College of Printing, 1958–76. Has designed over 300 posters, many of them classics. One of the very few native-born pioneers of British graphic design. Uses graphic means, frequently with humour, rather than photographic.

Robert Heritage CBE (1927–). *Furniture designer.* Born Birmingham. Birmingham College of Art 1942–46, RCA 1948–51 under R. D. Russell. Staff designer for G. W. Evans, furniture manufacturer, 1951–53. Freelance since 1953, designing furniture and lighting for UK and foreign firms. Consultant for Archie Shine, Concord/Rotaflex, Race, etc. Professor of Furniture Design RCA 1974–85. His frequently innovative designs, particularly for light fittings, have won him more Design Council awards than any other individual.

1964

Hardy Amies CVO (1909–). *Dress designer.* Trainee at W. & T. Avery, Birmingham 1930–34. Managing director Lachasse, London 1934–39. Founded his own dressmaking business 1946. Couturier-designer, very successful in marketing the look of the classic English understatement in his clothes and accessories for both men and women. Consultant to manufacturers in UK, EEC, US, Canada, Australia, New Zealand, Japan, Korea. Dressmaker to Her Majesty the Queen.

Alan Irvine (1926–). *Architect, exhibition and interior designer.* Studied architecture in London. RCA 1951–54. Worked with BBPR Group, Milan 1954–56. Private practice London from 1956 (as Buzas & Irvine since 1965). Interiors for Lazards, S. Australian Government, *Queen Elizabeth II*; exhibitions (for V&A Museum, Tate Gallery, RA, British Council, Olivetti) such as *Horses of San Marco* 1979, *Great Japan Exhibition* 1981, *Treasures of Ancient Nigeria* 1983. Museum work includes Old Master Drawings Gallery, Windsor Castle 1965; Crown Jewels Display, Tower of London 1968; Treasuries at Winchester and Christ Church Cathedrals 1968; Heinz Gallery RIBA 1972; Cabinet War Rooms Museum 1984. Consultant designer to Olivetti, Milan and the Conran Foundation. First British exhibition designer to match Continental (particularly Italian) standards of elegance and imaginative simplicity.

Sir Alec Issigonis CBE FRS (1906–). *Car designer*. Born Smyrna, Turkey. Studied engineering at Battersea Polytechnic; then draughtsman with Rootes Motors 1933–36. Suspension engineer, Morris Motors 1936, rising to Chief Engineer. Subsequently Chief Engineer BMC 1957–61, Director of R&D 1961–72. Conceived three landmarks in car design: Morris Minor 1948; Mini Minor 1959 – perhaps the most radical departure from conventional car design ever made, influencing European cars for at least two decades, and still in production; and Morris 1100 of 1962.

1965

Herbert Spencer Dr RCA (1924–).
Typographer. Born London. Worked with London Typographic Designers 1946–47. Own practice since 1948. Taught at Central School 1949–55. Founder/editor of *Typographica* 1949–67. Consultant to Lund Humphries Printers 1950–75; director of Lund Humphries Publishers since 1969. Former consultant to Universities of Leeds and East Anglia, British Rail, and RIBA. Consultant to W. H. Smith, Tate Gallery, Imperial War Museum; member of PO Stamp Advisory Committee. Professor of Graphic Arts RCA 1978–85. Prolific designer (work ranging from books and art gallery catalogues to signs and railway timetables), author and teacher. Publications include *Design in Business Printing* (1952), *The Visible Word* (1968), *Pioneers of Modern Typography* (1969). Founded British post-war typography in the late 1940s and early 1950s.

Robert Welch MBE (1929–). *Product designer and silversmith*. Malvern School of Art, Birmingham College of Art, RCA. Started own workshop in Chipping Campden 1955. Consultant designer to Old Hall Tableware from 1955. Specialised in stainless steel design and items such as cutlery, enamel steel products, light fittings, door furniture, bathroom fittings, cast-iron cooking utensils. Scope now includes consultancies, silverware commissions (originally for institutions, through the Goldsmith's Company, now also for individuals); opened a shop in Chipping Campden for his own wares, 1968.

1966

Natasha Kroll (1914–). *Shop display and television designer*. Born Moscow, studied at Reimann School of Art, Berlin. Taught window display at Reimann School, London 1936–40. Store display manager for Rowntree 1940–42. Display manager for Simpson's of Piccadilly 1942–55. Joined BBC TV 1955, responsible for design of all talks programmes (Monitor, Panorama), music and science programmes. Senior designer 1956, designing for drama. Since 1966, freelance designer for BBC, Yorkshire and LWT, responsible for numerous drama and opera production. Also film designer since 1969. Has designed several exhibitions.

1968

Dr Alexander Moulton CBE (1920–).
Engineering designer. Born Stratford-upon-Avon. Studied engineering at Cambridge 1938–39, 1947–49. Worked in aero-engine research for Bristol Aeroplane Co. 1939–44. Joined the family firm of rubber manufacturers 1949–56, establishing research department. Founded Moulton Developments Ltd 1956, working mainly in field of vehicle suspension: Flexitor vehicle suspension 1957, rubber cone spring 1959, Hydrolastic 1962, Hydragas 1973, all sponsored by and adopted for BMC Mini, 1100, Metro, etc.; Moulton bicycle 1962; Moulton Safety Coach 1969; Alex Moulton bicycle 1983. His bicycle designs were the most radical (and contentious) change for sixty years, initiating a new approach to small wheels, and a new interest in bicycles as transport.

1969

Kenneth Grange CBE (1929–). *Industrial designer*. Born London. Willesden School of Arts & Crafts 1944–47. Architectural assistant to Bronek Katz & Vaughan 1949–50. Designer with George Bower 1950–52; Jack Howe 1952–58. Set up on his own 1958–71. Founder partner Pentagram since 1972. Influenced by the sculptural simplicity of German post-war design. Designer of Venner parking meter, Kodak Instamatic, Kenwood mixers, Parker 25; typewriters, sewing machines, etc. for the Japanese firm Maruzen; and the powercar exterior for BR's High Speed Train. Has been able to bring to everyday things a high quality of design with painstaking attention to detail.

Margaret Leischner (**1908–1970**). *Textile designer*. Born Dresden. Studied there, and Bauhaus Dessau 1927–30. Taught weaving there 1931. Designer of woven textiles at Deutschen Werkstätten 1931; head of weaving at Modeschule der Stadt Berlin 1932–36. Head designer to furnishing fabric manufacturers in Gateshead 1938–44. Consultant designer 1944–50 to R. Grey & Co. and Fothergill & Harvey (car upholstery and radio baffle cloth). Head of Weaving Department RCA 1948–63. Designed Tintawn sisal carpet range 1959; consultant to Chemstrand for their Acrilan fibres.

Ian Proctor (**1918–**). *Small-boat designer*. Began designing boats, with no formal training, in 1948. First designs were high-performance racing dinghies. 52,000 boats have been produced from over 100 of his sailing-boat designs (Tempest class, 11-foot injection-moulded Topper, 16-foot Wayfarer, sailing surfboard Minisail, small weekend cruiser Nimrod, family racing boat Kestrel). In 1959 founded a mast design and manufacturing company.

Mary Quant OBE (**1934–**). *Fashion designer*. Born London. Studied illustration at Goldsmith's College. With her husband, designed hats for a leading miliner. Set up first shop, Bazaar, 1955, selling clothes designed and made by her. Now a design house, working with manufacturers. Her clothing, emphasizing youth, fun and colour, makes high fashion widely available. The environment of the store, designed to make shopping an agreeable experience, is an essential part of the retailing process. An international fashion entrepreneur continually extending her range, now including wall and furniture coverings, carpets, light fittings, toys, mugs, household goods. Associated with the miniskirt of the 1960s.

1970

David Gentleman (**1930–**). *Graphic designer and painter*. Studied at St. Albans School of Art 1947–8, and Royal College of Art 1950–53. His work cuts across the conventional distinctions between graphic design, illustration, print-making and painting, and has ranged in scale from postage stamps to the platform-length murals on the Underground at Charing Cross. He has drawn and designed for publishers here and in the United States, engraved the covers for the New Penguin Shakespeare, and published many lithographs of buildings and landscape. He has designed architectural wall-charts for the RIBA, graphic and photographic posters for London Transport and the National Trust, and historical panels for Westminster Abbey. He recently published two books of watercolours and critical commentary, on Britain and on London. He has always worked on his own.

Allen Hutt (**1901–1973**). *Newspaper designer*. Read history at Cambridge 1919–23. Joined *Daily Herald*, and was closely involved in establishment of *Workers' Weekly*. From 1929 was with *The Sunday Worker* and its successor *Daily Worker* as chief sub-editor. In 1935 redesigned *Reynold's News*, using his typographic knowledge to quietly revolutionise newspaper presentation. This brought him in contact with Stanley Morison and into the Monotype Corporation as newspaper consultant 1936–39. Adviser to many newspapers (*The Guardian, The Scotsman, Daily Herald, Irish Times, Der Spiegel, The Jewish Chronicle, The Calcutta Statesman*). Regarded typography not as an art form but as a disciplined instrument of communication.

1971

Gerald Benney (**1930–**). *Silversmith*. Born Hull. Trained as silversmith at Brighton College of Art, under Dunstan Pruden, then the RCA. Set up workshop 1955. Consultant to Viners Ltd 1957–70, designing for quantity production. Started making the collection of civic plate for Reading Corporation 1963 (250 pieces to date). Discovered technique of texturing 1964 – now generally adopted. Producing range of Beenham enamels since 1970, applying enamel directly to large areas of silver. Professor of Silversmithing RCA 1974–83.

Ronald Carter (**1926–**). *Furniture designer*. Interior design at Birmingham College of Art, furniture at RCA, winner of RCA silver medal (one student chair adopted for RCA's senior common room, another for London Airport). Worked in US before setting up UK consultancy in 1954; taught at RCA 1956–74. Has designed production furniture using modern factory techniques for Stag, Consort, Habitat and Peak; and pieces which combine hand-making with machine methods for Gordon Russell, and currently for Miles/Carter which he founded with Peter Miles in 1980. Recent projects for the BBC, V&A, Tate Gallery, and Terminal Four at Heathrow.

Jocelyn Herbert (**1917–**). *Stage and film designer*. Born London. Studied painting at André Lhôte's Studio, Paris 1932–33, and Slade 1934–36. Trained as stage designer at London Theatre Studio 1936–37. Resident stage designer, English Stage Co., Royal Court Theatre 1956–58. Freelance, largely based at Royal Court, 1958–68. Also worked for Old Vic, RSC, National Theatre, Metropolitan Opera New York, and Paris Opera. Films include *Tom Jones, Isadora, If, Ned Kelly, O Lucky Man*. Attracted to minimal settings with a few key elements, usually realistically based, preferably of authentic materials.

Richard Levin OBE (**1910–**). *Television designer*. Born London. Studied painting Slade and Paris. Apprenticed to Gaumont-British as stage and film designer 1928. Freelance 1931–39 (exhibition, interior, industrial design). Designed Army exhibitions during World War II. Resumed private practice 1945. Festival of Britain 1951 (The Land travelling exhibition). Joined BBC as Head of Design 1953–71, covering scenic design and construction, graphics, costume, make-up, special effects. Developed design policy for news, current affairs, light entertainment. Photographer since 1975. Author of *Television by Design*.

Neville Ward (**1922–**). *Interior designer*. Trained at School of Architecture Liverpool University, and Edinburgh College of Art. Private practice Ward & Austin (now Ward Associates) since 1948. Designed original façade for Design Centre Haymarket and Thames-side restaurant at Festival of Britain; Sealink ferries, ss *Oriana* and other ship interiors. Has also designed numerous exhibitions, and handled product design from pianos to decorative laminates.

1972

Tony Abbott MC (1921–). *Television and stage designer.* Studied at AA 1946–51. Between 1952–54 worked with LCC Architects Department (schools, exhibitions, housing), with Austin Smith & Partners (shops, factories), and with Wakeham (new Kuwait hotels, palaces, housing). Joined BBC TV 1954 as designer, 1962–80 senior designer (drama, opera, films, light entertainment). Freelance from 1981 working on films and opera. Prolific output of varied assignments.

Alan Fletcher (1931–). *Graphic designer.* Studied graphic design at Central School 1950–51, RCA 1953–56. Yale University 1956–57. Worked in US; upon returning to UK 1959, co-founded Fletcher/Forbes/Gill (working for Pirelli, Cunard, Olivetti, Reuters). Founder member of Pentagram 1972, a multi-discipline design group covering letterheads to interior design, product design to posters. His international reputation as a graphic designer is reflected in the gold awards he has received from the Designers and Art Directors Association and the New York "One Show". In 1977, he shared with Colin Forbes the Designers and Art Directors Association President's Award for outstanding contributions to design. The Society of Industrial Artists and Designers awarded him the 1982 Medal for outstanding achievement in industrial design.

Eileen Gray (1878–1976). *Architect, interior, furniture and textile designer.* Born Enniscorthy, Co. Wexford. Studied painting and drawing at Slade 1898–1902, and Paris 1902–05; lacquer work and furniture making with Sugawara, Paris 1907–14. Worked in Paris and S. France as independent furniture and interior designer from 1908, textile designer from 1910, architect from 1926. Work ranged from lacquer work to avant-garde concerns with chromed tubular metal and glass, aluminium and steel rod. Ran her own gallery 1922–30. Moved in the circle of Modern Movement architects, but they found her, not she, them. Her advanced and innovative designs, with their original approach to unexpected materials, were rediscovered in the 1960s.

Jean Muir CBE (1933–). *Fashion designer.* Born London. Worked as salesgirl and sketcher, Liberty's couture shop 1950–56. Designer for Jaeger 1956–63. Established Jane & Jane 1963–66. Founder, director, owner, head designer for Jean Muir Ltd since 1966. Sells in over 20 countries. Preference for classic, modest, sculptural clothes. Regards herself as a craftswoman as well as a designer.

Marianne Straub OBE (1909–). *Textile designer.* Born Switzerland. Trained in Zurich 1928–31. Worked in Swiss cotton mill, then studied machine production at Bradford Technical College 1932. Ethel Mairet's workshop 1933. Employed by Rural Industries Bureau 1934–37 to design for Welsh woollen industry; fabrics used by Gordon Russell, etc. Head designer for Helios Ltd 1937–50. Designer for Warner & Sons 1950–70; also for Tamesa Fabrics and Heal's Fabrics. Has designed fabrics for the liners *Queen Mary* (post-war refit) and *Caronia*, etc., London Transport (trains and buses), British Airways (Trident upholstery), Savoy Hotel, British Embassy (Paris), American Embassy cinema, etc. Taught at Central School, RCA, etc. Now freelancing (Jacquard furnishings, etc). Her early craft training influenced her approach to machine production.

1973

Noel London (1925–). *Engineering and product designer.* Born Mallow, Co. Cork. Central School 1952–55. GEC staff industrial designer 1955–60; set up internal consultancy group for in-house products. Industrial design partnership with Howard Upjohn 1960–80, then (after Upjohn's death) with Leslie Stokes and Will Bentall formed a multi-discipline design group. Specialising in capital goods and scientific instruments, has designed several ranges of fork-lift truck for Lansing Ltd, a full range of advanced microscopes for Vickers, and the whole field of computer equipment and interiors for ICL.

George Mackie DFC (1920–). *Graphic designer.* Dundee College of Art 1937–40, Edinburgh College of Art 1946–48. Freelance 1949–55 (illustration, publicity, packaging, exhibitions; for BBC publi-

cations, British Transport Hotels, POSB, National Trust for Scotland, several publishers). 1956–80 Head of Design at Gray's School of Art, Aberdeen, while continuing to freelance. From 1950, responsible for book design (typography, bindings, jackets, illustrations) and publicity at Edinburgh University Press.

Richard Stevens (1924–). *Industrial designer.* Born Dorking. Designer-technician with Siemens Electric Lamps and Supplies 1945–52. Lighting equipment designer with Metropolitan Vickers 1952–54. Designer with Atlas Lighting 1954–58, chief designer 1958–63. In 1960 received three Design Centre Awards in the fields of street lighting, display lighting and decorative lighting. Worked also for Ferguson Radio. Industrial design manager with STC 1968–69 and eventually responsible for industrial design co-ordination for all companies in ITT Europe. Design manager, Post Office Telecommunications, later British Telecom 1969–83. As well as co-ordinating the design of equipment, masterminded the visual identity programme for the new business. Believes a wholly objective approach to design in any field is not really possible; subjective judgement, concern for quality and personal conviction are the designer's real contribution, disciplined by an essential concern for the requirements of the design brief.

Walter Tracy (1914–). *Type designer.* Apprentice compositor Wm Clowes 1930–35. Typographic studio Baynard Press 1935–38. Notley Advertising 1938–46. Worked part-time with James Shand and Robert Harling for their publishing venture Art & Technics 1947. In charge of typographic development for (British) Linotype 1947–73, Linotype-Paul 1973–78. Has designed several well-used newspaper types (Jubilee 1953, Telegraph-Modern 1969, Times Europa 1972) and types for classified advertisements (Adsans 1959, Maximus 1967). Other types include Hebrew and Arabic designs. Author of *Letters of Credit; a view of type design* (1986).

Howard Upjohn (1925–1980). *Industrial designer.* Studied at Central School. Worked with Rank Precision 1953–55; Thorn Electrical 1955–57; Industrial Liaison Officer for Design Council 1957–60. Formed industrial design partnership with Noel London 1960. Specialised in scientific equipment. Designed radar for Plessey, gyro compass and Imacon high-speed camera for John Hadland, a range of spectrophotometers for Pye Unicam.

1974

Edward Ardizzone CBE RA (1900–1979). *Illustrator.* Born Haiphong, French Indo-China, of French-Italian father and Scottish-English mother. Came to England in his infancy. Did clerical work with various firms, then Eastern Telegraph Co. Evening classes at Westminster and Central School. Gave up clerical work 1926, designing book jackets, and starting to produce drawings for (eventually) almost 200 books, for 30 of which he was also author (starting with *Little Tim and the Brave Sea Captain* 1936). War artist World War II. His portrait of English life was "an unruffled vision of town, beach and country populated by fubsy matrons, cooks like cottage loaves, dozy mongrels, pointy-feet children and men who in general seem to be off-duty." An unmalicious Rowlandson.

David Carter CBE (1927–). *Industrial designer.* Apprenticed in plastics industry 1944–46. Product design at Central School 1948–51. Designer with Radiation Ltd 1951–55, chief designer Revo Electric 1955–60. Set up DCA consultancy 1960 in Warwick (industrial, engineering, electronic and graphic design). Major commissions include a range of tools for Stanley, telephones for British Telecom, vending machines for Mars, car interiors for Talbot/Peugeot, tube stock for London Transport, Electra High Speed Train for BR (scheduled for October 1989), Tangara Train for Sydney, New South Wales.

Hulme Chadwick (1910–1977). *Architect and industrial designer.* Studied at Manchester School of Art, RCA 1931–34. Architectural assistant in Manchester and London until 1938; Chief Camouflage Officer, Air Ministry 1938–44. Some of his

ten dummy aircraft factories were heavily bombed. Also responsible for the concealment of radar stations. Own practice from 1945 designing aircraft interiors (BOAC, A. V. Roe), exhibitions (Shell Chemicals, Festival of Britain), interiors for *Daily Mirror*, International Wool Secretariat, BR; particularly active in industrial design, most famous for a range of gardening products for Wilkinson Sword.

Colin Forbes (1928–). *Graphic designer.* Born London. Studied typography and graphic design at Central School 1948–51. Assistant to Herbert Spencer 1952–53. Freelance 1953–57. Art director Stuart's Advertising 1957–58. Head of Graphic Design, Central School 1958–60. Freelance from 1960; partner Fletcher/Forbes/Gill 1962–65; partner Crosby/Fletcher/Forbes 1965–72; partner Pentagram since 1972, currently working at the New York office. From 1972 he was a member of the British Design Council, in 1973 he was elected Royal Designer for Industry by the Royal Society of Arts and from 1976 to 1979 he served as International President of the Alliance Graphique Internationale. In 1977 he shared with Alan Fletcher the President's Award of the Designers and Art Directors Association in London for his outstanding contribution to design. Colin Forbes is past President of the American Institute of Graphic Arts.

Margaret Hall OBE (1936–). *Exhibition designer.* Born London. Studied textiles at Bromley (now Ravensbourne) College of Art 1954–57; interior design at RCA 1957–60. Design assistant to Casson Condor & Partners 1960–61 (university interiors); Bryan and Norman Westwood, Piet & Partners 1961–63 (university and shop interiors); Dennis Lennon & Partners 1963–64 (exhibitions, hotel and restaurant interiors). Set up British Museum Design Office 1964, designing major temporary exhibitions 1964–79, including ten opening exhibitions at Museum of Mankind 1970, Treasures of Tutankhamun 1972, Nomad and City (Museum of Mankind) 1976. Head of Design from 1980, with overall responsibility for design (at both BM and M of M) of public areas, permanent galleries, temporary exhibitions, publicity material. Most recent projects: entrance hall at BM; author of *On Display: a Design Grammar for Museum Exhibitions* (1986).

Lynton Lamb (1907–1977). *Book designer and illustrator.* Born Hyderabad. Studied painting and printmaking at Central School (1927–30). Joined OUP 1930, beginning 40 years of association, first redesigning bindings of bibles and prayer books (over 50 of each in print) then jackets for World's Classics, etc., as well as book designs. Began illustration 1929 with wood engravings for Shakespeare Head Press, then Fulcram Press and Golden Cockerel Press. Executed series of architectural decorations for Orient liners 1935–50. After World War II was art editor for Oxford Illustrated Trollope, designing the books and choosing illustrators. Also illustrated books for Limited Edition Club and Folio Society, and (in the 1950s) drew for *Radio Times*. Designed stamps for GPO 1955 and 1957. Head of Lithography, Slade 1950–71. His work as a painter was never far from his illustration, which was in a very English tradition.

Douglas Scott (1913–). *Industrial designer.* Studied silversmithing and jewellery at Central School 1926–29. Joined Osler & Faraday, electric light-fitting manufacturers 1929–33. Chief designer to GVD Illuminators 1933–36 (illumination engineers). Worked at Raymond Loewy's London office 1936–39, de Havilland Aircraft 1939–45. Set up own practice and Central School's pioneering industrial design department 1946. In 1953 designed London Transport's Routemaster bus – definitive version of their open entry buses; in early 1960s, GPO's callbox fittings, telephone and accessories. Other clients include Marconi, Ideal Standard, ITT, English Electric Computers, Potterton, Prestige, Shires Bathroom Equipment. His work is deliberately restrained and impersonal.

Peter Simpson (1921–). *Textile designer.* Duncan of Jordanstone College of Art Dundee 1947–50, then worked in US for three years. Chief designer (later design director) Donald Bros Dundee 1953–74, designing textiles for international furniture companies (Knoll, Hermann Miller, Jens Risom, Jack Lenor Larsen, Gordon Russell, HK, Race). Commissions included drapes and bedspreads for St. Catherine's College Oxford (with Arne Jacobson); fabrics for *Oriana, Transvaal Castle, Queen Elizabeth II*, and walls of Queen's Picture Gallery. Joined Marquess of Bute 1974 as company director to produce international collection of wool fabrics from the Scottish islands, working with Hermann Miller, Knoll, Fritz Hausen etc. and providing fabrics for many prestigious contracts such as Heathrow's Terminal 4 and the Westminster Centre by Powell & Moya. Winner of five design awards.

1975

Gordon Cullen CBE (1914–). *Architect-draughtsman and planner.* Born Yorkshire. Architecture and draughtsmanship at Regent Street Polytechnic 1930–32. During the 1930s worked as assistant in various offices (Raymond McGrath, Godfrey Samuel, Tecton). Writer and illustrator for Architectural Press 1946–56, following its editorial policy of translating seventeenth-century English landscape design into an urban context. Notable propagandist for the natural English informal approach to planning. Consultant 1959–62 to development plans for Delhi, Calcutta, Liverpool, Bolton, Northampton. Consultant to Buckinghamshire County Council 1965 on development of villages; since then has been planner or consultant for proposals at Llantrisant, Tenterden, Peterborough, Ware, Telford, Isle of Dogs, Glasgow City Centre.

Eileen Diss (1931–). *TV, stage and film designer.* Studied at Central School. Worked for BBC TV 1952–59, moving up from children's programmes to the Sunday Play. Since 1959 has freelanced, mainly for TV, but also for stage productions and films. Programmes include Maigret series and many Plays of the Month for BBC; also operas and operettas. Designed National Theatre production of *The Caretaker* among others.

1976

Lionel Haworth OBE (1912–). *Engineering designer.* Born in Orange Free State, S. Africa. Studied Engineering at University of Capetown. Apprenticed with AEC

Hulme Chadwick

Southall 1934–36 (lorries and buses). Joined Rolls-Royce 1936 as designer, rising to Chief Engineer Turbo-props 1962. Worked on Merlin Marine engines; designed WR1, RR's first jet engine; established the design concept of the 3-shaft axial-flow RCA3 (a concept used in service 30 years later in the RB 211); worked on Trent first turbo-prop to fly; designed Dart, first turbo-prop to enter service; Tyne, still the world's most fuel-efficient subsonic aero propulsion system. Responsible for all Bristol-Siddeley engines as Chief Designer after 1964, including the Olympus for TSR2 and (particularly) Concorde; and RB199, the RAF's major engine today.

Zandra Rhodes (**1940–**). *Fashion and textile designer*. Born Chatham. Studied textile printing and lithography at Medway College of Art 1959–61; printed textiles at RCA 1961–64. Set up print factory and studio 1964–66. Produced dresses using own prints 1966. Freelance 1968–75, designing own collection for UK and US, also furnishings and wallpaper. Formed Zandra Rhodes UK Ltd 1974. Opened first shop 1975. Pursues a particular mood of English fantasy, and has achieved worldwide recognition.

Hans Schmoller (**1916–1985**). *Typographer*. Born Berlin. Apprentice compositor Berlin 1933–37, part-time studies in calligraphy and lettering. From the Monotype School 1937 became assistant manager, Morija Printing Works, Basutoland 1938–46. Assistant to Oliver Simon, Curwen Press 1947–49. Joined Penguin Books as typographer 1949, taking over from Jan Tschichold; head of production 1956, consultant 1976–80. Maintained and developed Tschichold's standards in a time of diversification and expansion; also directed Pelican History of Art and Buildings of England series from their conception. His typography for *The Complete Pelican Shakespeare* welds together editorially complex material. Also designed for Allen Lane and (as freelance) other publishers. With his practical knowledge and German background of craft tradition, ''Half-point'' Schmoller was the ideal successor to Tschichold. The conern for detail and precision seen in quality German printing

was brought to mass-produced paperbacks, resulting in a distinction unusual in British books of any kind.

1977
Dr W. C. Brown OBE (**1928–**). *Bridge designer*. Studied at University College Southampton, and Imperial College (diploma 1951). Joined consulting engineers Freeman Fox & Partners, principal designer 1960, partner 1970. Principal designer of bridges for Volta River 1956, Forth Road 1964, Severn and Wye 1966, Auckland Harbour 1969, Erskine 1971, Bosporus 1973, Avonmouth 1975, Humber 1980. His innovative designs, deriving from a search for better and simpler ways of using steel, result in efficient and elegant structures and large cost savings. Has also designed radio telescopes in Australia and Canada, cranes and other heavy load-bearing structures.

George Him (**1900–1982**). *Graphic designer*. Born Lodz, Poland. Studied Roman Law at Moscow University, Comparative Religion at Bonn, and art at Leipzig. Freelance in Germany 1928, returned to Poland and set up Lewitt-Him partnership with Jan Le Witt which lasted 20 years. Came to London 1937. They produced many posters, particularly during World War II, and illustrated books, especially for children, sometimes also writing them. Designed the Guinness clock for Festival of Britain 1951, exhibitions (Masada 1966, Israel Pavilion Expo 67). Was consultant to El Al for many years. Designed covers for *The New Middle East*, etc. Was discoverer, with Stephen Potter, of the county of Schweppshire 1951–64. Did illustrations for children's TV. His work was witty and humorous, with almost childlike fantasy. Beneath its gaiety and apparent spontaneity it was serious and immensely professional.

Julia Trevelyan Oman CBE (**1930–**). *Stage and film designer*. Studied interior design at RCA. Worked for BBC TV 1955–67; her many designs include *Alice in Wonderland* 1966. Theatre work for National, RSC, Vienna, Royal Opera, Royal Ballet, Hamburg State Opera, Glyndebourne, Royal Opera Stockholm. Exhibition design for National Portrait Gallery and Madame Tussaud's. Her designs always show immense care for detail. Wide range of work from Jonathan Miller's *Merchant of Venice* with Olivier, Ashton's ballet *Enigma Variations*, Glyndebourne's *Arabella*, to Alan Bennett's *Getting On*.

A. A. Rubbra CBE (1903–1982).

Engineering designer. Born Northampton. Trained Bristol University. Joined Rolls-Royce 1925 as development engineer. Chief Designer 1940. Technical Director 1954 (covering all products: cars, aero engines, nuclear power). Deputy Chairman of the Nuclear Division, 1959. Chief Technical Adviser 1966. Retired 1968, remaining a consultant until 1976. Worked on the R engine (which won Schneider Trophy). Most important work was on design of Merlin and supervision of all wartime design work on its vital range: on Griffon and on Eagle. Heavily involved in design during gas turbine development (1945–65). Involved in design of Conway, first by-pass jet, and advised on Concorde engine. His design contributions were sometimes daring but always sound.

1978
Jon Bannenberg (1929–). *Yacht designer*. Born Australia. Studied at Sydney Conservatorium of Music. Founded London design company 1954. Later in partnership with Frank Partridge & Sons, antiquaries, designing houses, interiors. Exhibitions at the Louvre and V&A Museum. Predominant design activities since 1965 large yachts: over 120 both sail and motor constructed worldwide, to include Holland, Italy, France, Germany, Finland, Greece, USA, Japan and Australia. Has reputation for outstandingly meticulous and innovative design, especially in the co-ordination of hull, superstructure and interior spaces.

Bill Brandt (1904–1983). *Photographer*. Born London, parents of Russian descent. Educated mainly in Germany and Switzerland. Never went to photography school, but worked as pupil with Man Ray, Paris 1929–30, learning the value of experiment and surrealism. Learnt technique and printing by experience. Freelance social documentary photographer London 1931–39 (*Weekly Illustrated*, *Picture Post*, *Verve*, etc). Photographer for *Lilliput*

1939–45; worked on photographic surveys of bomb shelters for Home Office; also photography for National Buildings Record. Freelance since 1945. His photographs up to 1945 – the English at home (poor and rich, north and south) and at war, English landscapes, English townscapes – have become indelible images of social observation. His work since 1945 includes portraits of writers and artists, landscapes, and poetic abstractions of the human form. All his work is imbued with a haunting or surreal presence.

Geoffrey Harcourt (1935–). *Furniture designer*. Born London. Studied at High Wycombe School of Art, and RCA 1957–60. Worked in Chicago (with Latham, Tyler, Jensen) and Copenhagen (Jacob Jensen) 1960–61. Started own one-man practice London 1961, concentrating on furniture. Contracted to Artifort, Holland from 1962 for design of seating. Twenty or so programmes of furniture currently in production by Artifort and others, and under license in Japan. His chairs much used in airports.

Lord Snowdon GCVO (1930–). *Photographer*. Designed the Aviary at London Zoo 1965; also electrically propelled chair for disabled people, sets for Cranko's *Keep Your Hair On*, a collection of ski clothes; creator of TV films. Artistic adviser to *Sunday Times* and Sunday Times Publications since 1962. Photo-journalist of great professionalism and perceptiveness, with work for *Sunday Times*, *Vogue*, etc. Has also compiled ten books of his photographs.

1979
Colin Chapman CBE (1928–1982). *Car designer*. Studied engineering at London University. Structural engineer 1951, civil and development engineer with British Aluminium 1952. Formed Lotus Cars 1955. First sports car was an Austin 7 converted by him into a trials car. Expanded from lock-up garages in Muswell Hill to purpose-built factory with test track, Norfolk 1976. Produced both production sports cars (Elite 1959, Elan 1963, Europa 1966, Esprit 1976) and racing cars (Formula 1 Lotus 25, 1962; 33, 1965; 72, 1970s). Introduced use of lightweight structures, aerodynamics and other

aerospace techniques into the design of racing and road cars. Elan and Europa both used fibreglass bodies. Dynamic and original thinker, but later less successful as a businessman.

Paul Hogarth (**1917–**). *Illustrator.* Born Kendal. Manchester College of Art, St. Martin's School of Art. Watercolours and drawings based on his world travels are published in his own books, or in collaboration with other writers (Brendan Behan, Robert Graves, Graham Greene). Has also illustrated other books and magazines and designed many jackets for Penguin (Graham Greene novels from 1962, revised Penguin Shakespeare from 1979). Designed stamps for PO 1984, 1985. Taught at RCA 1964–71. A sharp observer of the scene around him: personification of the artist-as-reporter, with a very fluent style.

Sir Osbert Lancaster (**1908–1986**). *Illustrator.* Read English at Oxford, studied art at Byam Shaw, Ruskin and Slade schools. Abandoned easel painting early, concentrating on murals and illustration. Designed posters for London Transport. Joined *AR* 1934–39 as writer. His books, *Progress at Pelvis Bay* 1936, *Pillar to Post* 1938, *Homes Sweet Homes* 1939, *Draynflete Revealed* 1949, definitively documented the architectural scene with wit and perception. *Classical Landscape With Figures* 1947 is a scholarly, funny and wonderfully illustrated book on Greece. Invented the pocket cartoon (for *Daily Express*) 1939. Creator of Maudie Littlehampton, for over 30 years a sharp and outraged commentator on society around her (and us). Also designed for opera and ballet.

1980

Dennis Bailey (**1931–**). *Graphic designer.* Born Bognor Regis. West Sussex School of Art 1946–51, RCA 1951–53. Assistant editor *Graphis*, Zurich 1956. Freelance designer and illustrator 1957–60 (CoID, Worshipful Company of Goldsmiths, Time Life), also taught typography at Central School 1959–60. Lived and worked Paris 1960–64 as freelance designer and art director in advertising and publishing. Art director *Town* magazine 1964–66. Design and illustration practice London since 1967

(Penguin, *Nova*, *The Economist*, *The Listener*, Arts Council, RIBA, British Council, Tate Gallery, Thomson Organisation). Work includes catalogues, posters, exhibition graphics (Picasso's Picassos 1981, Genius of Venice 1983, Renoir 1985), stamps, books etc. Taught graphic design at Chelsea School of Art 1970–81 and currently at Middlesex Polytechnic.

1981

Quentin Blake (**1932–**). *Illustrator.* Read English at Cambridge, then studied part-time at Chelsea School of Art. Freelance illustrator since 1957, drawing covers for *The Spectator*, cartoons for *Punch*, illustrations and cartoons for other magazines such as *The Listener*; also designing book jackets. Began illustrating children's books 1960; has since illustrated well over 100, some written by himself. Has also illustrated books for adults (Aristophanes' *The Birds*, *The Hunting of the Snark*, *Animal Farm*). Has taught at RCA since 1965 (Head of Illustration Department 1978–86).

Nicholas Butler (**1942–**). *Industrial designer.* Leeds College of Art. RCA 1963–66. USA IBM fellowship under the guidance of Eliott Noyes, then in London at GLC as co-project leader Industrialised Building Systems. Founding partner BIB Design Consultants 1967. Design work of BIB includes all Decca Marine radar and navigational products from 1969–1983. Ohmeda (BOC) medical products including operating theatre equipment. Dunhill pens and watches. Minolta cameras, including Minolta 7000, voted European camera of the year 1985. Award winning Duracell torch range. Ferguson 1986 range of televisions, etc.

Matthew Carter (**1937–**). *Type designer.* Trained as punch cutter and typefounder at Enschede. Cut replacement punches for OUP's Fell collection. Freelance designer 1957–63. Typographic adviser to Crosfield Electronics 1963–65 (characters for Lumitype photosetter). Staff type designer Linotype New York 1965–71. Freelance London 1971, continuing work for Linotype (types for photo and digital composition). Co-founder of Bitstream Inc, Massachusetts (fonts for computerised image-setting). Typographic adviser to HMSO 1980–84.

Type designs include Snell Roundhand, Cascade Script, Helvetica Compressed, Olympian, Video, Shelley Script, Galliard, Bell Centennial, and several exotics. Has also drawn alphabets for London Airport signs, Lucas, Nissan.

Martin Hunt (**1942–**). *Ceramics and glass designer.* Gloucestershire College of Art 1960–63, RCA 1963–66. Formed Queensberry Hunt design group 1966. Winner of four Design Council Awards including one, jointly with James Kirkwood, for ceramic lamps. He has worked for Hornsea Pottery, Bing & Grondahl, Wedgwood, Rosenthal, Thomas Glass, Watson's Potteries, Doulton, Ravenhead, Judge International and Pilkington Glass. Was elected to the Faculty of Royal Designers for Industry 1981 and was Head of the Department of Glass RCA 1976–86.

1982

Bernard Lodge (**1933–**). *Graphic designer.* Studied graphic design RCA 1956–59. Joined BBC TV Graphic Design section 1960–67 Work included the first five title sequences for *Doctor Who*, some involving an early use of the slit-scan process. Designer/director for Streich-Fletcher-Perkins 1967–69. Returned to BBC 1970–77. Freelance 1977–79. Partner and designer/director Lodge/Cheesman Productions 1979–86. Now a freelance consultant.

Derek Prime (**1932–**). *Engineering design.* Studied at N. Staffordshire Technical College. Apprenticed to Thomas Bolton & Sons, Staffordshire 1948–54. Joined JCB Research as Designer 1954, progressing to Chief Designer, Technical Director and Managing Director in 1973. The company manufactures earthmoving and materials-handling equipment with a reputation for reliability, performance, concern for the operator and rugged good looks. Products include backhoe-loaders, track-mounted excavators, articulated loading shovels and telescopic rough terrain materials handling machines.

1983

Derek Birdsall (1934–). *Graphic designer.* Born Knottingley, Yorkshire. Wakefield College of Art, Central School. Was the 'B' of BDMW, design partnership closely connected with Balding + Mansell printers. He designed the first Pirelli calendar 1964, has worked for Lotus, Morphy Richards, Dorothy Gray, United Overseas Bank in Singapore, Japan Airlines, Penguin, American Express. Has been art director of *Nova, Twen, Town, Connoisseur*; is now art director of Mobil's *Pegasus* magazine. Consultant to Mobil and United Technologies, designing and producing Mobil-sponsored Gallery Guides for V&A Museum, plus books on arts and crafts of the world. Has designed catalogues and exhibits for National Museum of American Folk Art New York, Library of Congress, Museum of Fine Arts Boston, and a catalogue for the Louvre. Has taught at London College of Printing, Central School and RCA. A disciplined designer/typographer.

Ted Happold (1930–). *Engineering designer.* Born 1930. Studied Civil Engineering at Leeds University. Site engineer for Sir Robert McAlpine & Sons 1952–54; engineer for Ove Arup & Partners 1956–58, worked on Rising Hill School, Coventry Cathedral, Sydney Opera House. Severud, Elstad and Kruger, New York 1958–60. Senior Engineer, becoming Executive Partner, Structures 3, Ove Arup & Partners 1960–76. Worked on wide range of buildings including winning entry with Piano, Rice and Rogers for Centre Beaubourg Competition 1972. Since 1976 Professor of Building Engineering at University of Bath where architects and engineers are taught together. Leads team researching into design methods for long-span flexible structures. Senior Partner, Buro Happold, Consulting Engineers who have carried out civil, structural and environmental services engineering for a wide range of projects including among others the Mannheim Lattice Shell and an aviary for Munich Zoo in Germany; Council of Ministries, the Diplomatic Club, the British Embassy and the Riyadh City Centre in Saudi Arabia, Naaish Khana and the Cultural Centre in Baghdad, Tsim Sha Tsui Cultural Centre and Kowloon Park Sports Centre in Hong Kong; Baltimore Harbour Lights Theatre and Washington Symphony Orchestra in the USA and in Britain Worcester College, Oxford. In 1980, together with Sebire and Allsop, won the Vauxhall Cross Competition. In 1985 with Derek Walker Associates and John Bury came second in the Leeds Playhouse Competition. This year they assisted Trevor Denton of Denton, Tunley, Scott in their Aston University competition win and together with Feilden Clegg won the Iona Competition.

1984

Eileen Ellis (1933–). *Textile designer.* Leicester College of Art 1950–52, Central School 1952–54, RCA 1954–57. Worked for Ascher & Co. 1957–59, designing printed and woven fabrics for couture market and Marks & Spencer. Formed Orbit Design Group 1960. Designed fabrics for BEA Trident and throughout the fleet; proscenium curtains for a theatre in Birmingham; fabrics for Edinburgh Weavers, John Lewis, Morton Sundour, etc. Formed Weaveplan 1970 with Ann Bristow. Sole partner since 1975, with five designers. Has worked or is working for Irish Ropes (Tintawn) overseeing all carpet designs; C. & J. Hirst (furnishing fabrics); Vescom, Deurne, Holland (wall coverings); Abbotsford Fabrics; John Orr, Eire (upholstery fabrics); Jamasque (styling all fabric ranges).

Jacqueline Groag (1903–1986). *Textile designer.* Born Prague. Studied in Vienna. Moved to Paris 1937, designing dress prints for leading couturiers (Lanvin, Schiaparelli). Came to London 1939, designing dress and furnishing textiles. Broke away from stereotyped floral patterns of the time. Her designs appeared on wallpaper, laminates, carpets, Christmas cards, even Liberty book matches. Has worked for Edinburgh Weavers, Bond-Worth carpets, de la Rue, British Rail, Festival of Britain, etc.

Ralph Koltai CBE (1924–). *Stage designer.* Born Berlin of Hungarian descent. Came to England 1939. Graphic design evening classes Epsom School of Art 1942–44, stage design Central School 1948–51. Window displays for London stores 1951–53. Freelance stage designer from 1950, working almost exclusively on operas 1950–62 (Royal Opera, Sadlers Wells, Scottish Opera, National Welsh Opera, English Opera Group). Also designs for Ballet Rambert. Associate designer RSC 1963–66, and since 1976. Also worked for other theatres including National. Head of Theatre Design, Central School 1965–73. Very art-motivated, has experimented with wide variety of techniques; productions frequently rely on careful engineering as well as elegant sculptural form. Has designed over 150 operas, plays, ballets, at home and abroad.

1985

Michael Foreman (1938–). *Illustrator.* Studied at Lowestoft School of Art; St. Martin's; RCA 1960–63. Has since freelanced, illustrating magazines, books and advertising in UK and US. Worked for wide range of industrial clients (Mobil) and made animated films in UK and Scandinavia. Art editor of *Ambit* since 1963. Has illustrated innumerable books, especially for children, some of the latter being written by himself. A much-travelled illustrator of great versatility and sophistication.

Sir Frank Whittle OM KBE CB (1907–). *Engineering designer.* Born Coventry. Joined RAF 1923, attending many courses in engineering. Obtained patent for jet propulsion 1930. Sent by RAF to study engineering at Cambridge 1934–37. Remaining with RAF, was attached to Power Jets Ltd. to develop experimental gas turbines. Ground test unit (a very simple design appropriate to the technology of the time) ran 1937. First flown in Gloster E28/39, May 1941. Continued to direct work at Power Jets until 1946. Conceived addition of re-heat; gas turbine driving a propeller; ducted fan engine; by-pass engine. Retired from RAF 1948 (as Air Commodore). Continues in engineering (drilling machinery).

1986

Kay Cosserat (1947–). *Textile designer.* Textiles at Goldsmith's College 1966–70, RCA 1970–72. Developed an interest in knitting on flat-bed machines. Set up weave studio 1972. Knitted fabrics for James

Drew and Christian Dior. Soon supplemented her loom by flat-bed knitting machine. Cosserat Design Ltd formed 1966. Now designs and produces complete Cosserat range in her factory at Milton Keynes. Also has worked on commissions for firms such as Jaeger. Has an adventurous colour sense within the mainstream of fashion trends.

Marshall Meek (**1925–**). *Naval architect.* Born Auchtermuchty, Fife. Worked in Caledon Shipyard Dundee 1942–49. Studied naval architecture Glasgow University, graduating 1946. British Ship Research Association 1949–53. Naval architect with Alfred Holt (later, Ocean Transport & Trading) Liverpool 1953–78, designing and supervising new ships. Head of Ship Technology, British Shipbuilders, Newcastle-upon-Tyne 1979–84. Managing Director National Maritime Institute 1984. Deputy Chairman British Maritime Technology 1985. A key figure in modern innovatory ship design.

Alan Tye (**1933–**). *Industrial designer and architect.* Born London. Architecture at Regent Street Polytechnic 1952–60. Assistant to Arne Jacobsen, Copenhagen 1960–62. Private practice as designer since 1962. Designs include Meridian One sanitary fittings for Adamsez 1965; Modric series of architectural ironmongery for Allgood 1966 (the first comprehensive and integrated range in UK); office sign systems 1971; computer furniture for Apple 1980; cubicle systems 1981; prefabricated hotel room 1982; stainless steel hardware. Also designs for print, particular newspapers and technical information. His work is usually in fields related to his architectural training.

Selected Bibliography

Below is a list of general books of relevance to the activities of Royal Designers over the past fifty years', and catalogues of the most important mixed exhibitions including Royal Designers' work.

More detailed biographies and bibliographies for many RDIs are included in *Contemporary Designers*, edited by Ann Lee Morgan (London, Macmillan, 1984) and in *The Conran Directory of Design*, edited by Stephen Bayley (Octopus Conran, 1985). *A Bibliography of Design in Britain 1851–1970* by Anthony J. Coulson (Design Council, 1979) is also worth consulting.

The annual RDI Addresses have usually been printed in the relevant *Journal of the Royal Society of Arts*, and a selection of past addresses – *Royal Designers on Design* – has recently been published by the Design Council.

The Royal Society of Arts is in the process of compiling a record of the work of all Royal Designers for Industry, past, present and Honorary. The National Design Archive has substantial collections of papers and photographs of the work of a growing number of Royal Designers.

GENERAL BOOKS

Anscombe, Isabelle. *A Woman's Touch: Women in Design from 1860 to the Present Day*. Virago, 1984

Baynes, Ken. *Industrial Design and the Community*. Lund Humphries, 1967

Carrington, Noel. *Design in the Home*. Country Life, 1933
Design and Decoration in the Home, Country Life, 1938
Industrial Design in Britain. George Allen & Unwin, 1976

Carrington, Noel and Harris, Muriel, eds. *British Achievement in Design*, Pilot Press, 1946

Designers in Britain. Surveys of work by members of the Society of Industrial Artists. Wingate, 1947, 1949, 1951; Deutsch, 1953, 1957, 1964, 1971

Dowling, H. G. *A Survey of British Industrial Arts*. F. Lewis, 1935

Farr, Michael. *Design in British Industry – A Mid-Century Survey*. Cambridge University Press, 1955

Gloag, John. *Modern Publicity in War*. Studio, 1941

Gloag, John, ed. *Design in Modern Life*. Allen & Unwin, 1934

Glynn, Prudence. *In Fashion: Dress in the Twentieth Century*. George Allen & Unwin, 1978

Hamilton, Nicola, ed. *From Spitfire to Microchip: Studies in the History of Design from 1945*. Design Council, 1985

Holland, James. *Minerva at Fifty: The Jubilee History of the Society of Industrial Artists and Designers 1930–1980*. Hurstwood Publications, 1980

Holme, Geoffrey. *Industrial Design and the Future*. Studio, 1934

Levey, Michael. *London Transport Posters*. Phaidon, 1976

Lewis, John. *The Twentieth Century Book. Its illustration and design*, 1967, revised 1984. Herbert Press

MacCarthy, Fiona. *All Things Bright and Beautiful: Design in Britain 1830 to today*. George Allen & Unwin, 1972. Republished as *A History of British Design 1830–1970*, 1979
British Design since 1880. A Visual History. Lund Humphries, 1982

Maynard, Alister, ed. *The Value of Good Design*. Report on Scottish Design Congress, 1954. Council of Industrial Design, Glasgow, 1954

Middleton, Michael. *Group Practice in Design*. Architectural Press, 1967

Pevsner, Nikolaus. *An Enquiry into Industrial Art in England*. Cambridge University Press, 1937
Studies in Art, Architecture and Design, vol. 2. Thames & Hudson, 1968

Plummer, Raymond. *Nothing Need Be Ugly. The first 70 years of the Design and Industries Association*. DIA, 1985

Read, Herbert, intr. *The Practice of Design*. Lund Humphries, 1946

Russell, Gordon. 'The Work of the Royal Designers for Industry', Lecture to Design and Industries Association, reprinted *Journal of Royal Society of Arts*, 22 October 1948

Woodham, Jonathan. 'British Art in Industry in 1935'. Paper in *Design and Industry*. Design Council, 1980
The Industrial Designer and the Public. Pembridge Press, 1983

Young, Dennis and Barbara. *Furniture in Britain Today*. Alec Tiranti, 1964

Zeman, Zbynek. *Selling the War. Art and Propaganda in World War II*. Orbis, 1978

EXHIBITION CATALOGUES

Britain Can Make It. Exhibition Catalogue. London, Victoria and Albert Museum, 1946. Council of Industrial Design

Design 46. Illustrated survey of exhibits at *Britain Can Make It*. London, HMSO, 1946

Did Britain Make It? British Design in Context 1946–86. ed. Penny Sparke, book accompanying exhibition at Royal College of Art, London. Design Council, 1986

British Art and Design 1900–1960. Catalogue of C20th Gallery. London, Victoria and Albert Museum, 1983

British Art in Industry. London, Royal Academy, 1935

Design at Work: An Introduction to the Industrial Designer. RDI Exhibition, London, Royal Academy, 1948

Festival of Britain. Catalogue of Exhibits, South Bank Exhibition, London, HMSO, 1951
Design in the Festival. Illustrated Review of British Goods. Council of Industrial Design, 1951
A Tonic to the Nation. ed. Mary Banham and Bevis Hillier, book accompanying Festival of Britain exhibition. London, Victoria and Albert Museum, 1976. Thames & Hudson

Homespun to Highspeed: A Century of British Design 1880–1980. Sheffield City Art Galleries, 1979

1966 and All That: Design and the Consumer in Britain 1960–1969. ed. Jennifer Harris, Sarah Hyde and Greg Smith, book accompanying exhibition at Whitworth Art Gallery, Manchester. Trefoil, 1986

A New Design for Living. Design in British Interiors 1930–1951. London, B2 Gallery. Wapping, Lane Publications

"That's Shell – that is!" An Exhibition of Shell Advertising Art. London, Barbican Gallery, 1983

Thirties: British Art and Design Before the War. London, Hayward Gallery, 1979

Utility Furniture and Fashion, 1941–1951. London, Geffrye Museum, 1974

The Way We Live Now: Designs for Interiors 1950 to the Present Day. London, Victoria & Albert Museum, 1978

Index of RDIs